A Deep Dive Into The Top 50 Cryptocurrencies

A DYOR (Do Your Own Research) Guide

BY

Michael McNaught

An educational book for readers of all ages.

Interested in learning about Cryptocurrency?

Well, this is the book for you!

Copyright

A Deep Dive Into The Top 50 Cryptocurrencies

A DYOR (Do Your Own Research) Guide

Written By Michael McNaught

Copyright © 2023.

All Rights Reserved.

Preface

Hi there! My name is Michael McNaught, a scientist by profession, and an avid blockchain and crypto enthusiast. I enjoy learning about this amazing cutting-edge technology and sharing my knowledge with others. I got into cryptocurrency in 2021 and have progressed to building and operating mining rigs. Throughout my cryptocurrency journey, I have realized that only a very small percentage of individuals are actually knowledgeable about the fundamentals of blockchain technology and cryptocurrency.

As such, I set out to write '**Cryptocurrency Chronicles: Unlocking The Secrets Of Blockchain Technology**,' an easily understandable and comprehensive book that gives the reader a solid understanding of the basic concepts of blockchain technology and cryptocurrency. If you haven't read it, pick up your copy today!

A Deep Dive Into The Top 50 Cryptocurrencies: A DYOR Guide is a continuation of my previous book. As such, I will make the assumption that you are familiar with the fundamentals of blockchain technology and cryptocurrency.

If you are seeking a comprehensive DYOR guide on the top 50 cryptocurrencies? Well, look no further, this is the book for you!

I do hope that you learn something new, informative and valuable that will assist you in making sound crypto investment decisions. For purchasing this book, I thank you!

Table of Contents

Top 50 Cryptocurrencies:

A Deep Dive

-Poem

Oh, doing research on crypto,

Can sometimes make you go loco.

With all these coins to choose,

It's easy to get confused.

Bitcoin, Ethereum, Dogecoin too,

Which one should you choose to pursue?

Is it better to invest or mine?

Or maybe just buy on a dime?

But wait, there's more to know,

About the blockchain and how it flows.

Public or private, which is right?

And what about security, day or night?

With so much information to obtain,

You might think it's all in vain.

But fear not, my fellow crypto friend,

Your research will pay off in the end.

So keep on digging and learning,
And soon you'll have the knowledge burning.
To invest in crypto with great success,
And leave your financial worries in distress.

So go on, embrace the crypto craze,
And let your research guide your ways.
And who knows, maybe someday soon,
You'll be singing a different tune!

Chapter 1

Bitcoin (BTC)

Bitcoin is the world's first decentralized digital currency, which was created in 2009 by an unknown person or group under the pseudonym Satoshi Nakamoto. In this chapter, we will explore how Bitcoin works, how transactions are processed, and how the security of the Bitcoin network is maintained.

-The Bitcoin Network

The Bitcoin network is a decentralized peer-to-peer network, which means that there is no central authority or middleman controlling the network. Instead, transactions are processed and verified by network nodes called "miners," who are rewarded with newly created bitcoins for their work.

-How Transactions are Processed

When a user sends bitcoins to another user, the transaction is broadcast to the entire Bitcoin network. Miners then collect these transactions and add them to a "block" of transactions. Each block contains a unique code, called a "hash," which is generated by the miners based on the transactions in the block.

Once a block is generated, it is broadcast to the entire network, and other miners work to validate the transactions in the block. This process involves solving a complex mathematical puzzle, known as the "Proof of Work" algorithm. The first miner to solve the puzzle and validate the transactions in the block is rewarded with newly created bitcoins and fees from the transactions in the block.

-Security of the Bitcoin Network

The security of the Bitcoin network is maintained through the use of cryptography and the Proof of Work algorithm. Each transaction is verified using complex mathematical equations, which make it virtually impossible for anyone to tamper with the transactions.

Additionally, the Proof of Work algorithm ensures that the network is secure by making it extremely difficult and resource-intensive to generate new blocks. Miners must solve complex mathematical puzzles to validate transactions and generate new blocks, which requires a significant amount of computing power and energy.

-Bitcoin Wallets

Bitcoin wallets are digital wallets that store a user's private keys, which are used to access and transfer bitcoins. There are several types of Bitcoin wallets, including desktop wallets, mobile wallets, and hardware wallets.

Desktop and mobile wallets are software applications that run on a user's computer or mobile device, while hardware wallets are physical devices that store a user's private keys offline. Hardware wallets are considered to be the most secure type of Bitcoin wallet, as they are less vulnerable to hacking and cyberattacks.

In conclusion, Bitcoin is a decentralized digital currency that operates on a peer-to-peer network. Transactions are processed and validated by network nodes called miners, who are rewarded with newly created bitcoins for their work.

The security of the Bitcoin network is maintained through the use of cryptography and the proof of Work algorithm, which make it virtually impossible for anyone to tamper with the transactions.

Bitcoin wallets are digital wallets that store a user's private keys, which are used to access and transfer bitcoins. Understanding how Bitcoin works is essential for understanding the potential applications and limitations of blockchain technology.

Chapter 2

Ethereum (ETH)

Ethereum is a decentralized blockchain platform that allows developers to build and deploy decentralized applications (dApps). In this chapter, we will explore how Ethereum works, how it differs from Bitcoin, and the role of smart contracts in the Ethereum ecosystem.

-The Ethereum Network

Like Bitcoin, the Ethereum network is a decentralized peer-to-peer network. However, unlike Bitcoin, which was designed primarily as a digital currency, Ethereum is designed as a platform for building decentralized applications.

In addition to the blockchain, the Ethereum network includes a virtual machine, called the Ethereum Virtual Machine (EVM), which allows developers to write and execute code on the blockchain. The EVM is a Turing-complete machine, which means that any program that can be written in any other programming language can be written in Ethereum's Solidity programming language and executed on the EVM.

-How Transactions Are Processed

When a user sends a transaction on the Ethereum network, it is broadcast to the entire network and processed by miners, who validate the transaction and add it to the blockchain. Each transaction on the Ethereum network includes a "gas" limit and a "gas" price. Gas is the unit used to measure the computational effort required to execute a transaction or contract on the Ethereum network.

The gas limit is the maximum amount of gas that a user is willing to pay for the transaction, while the gas price is the amount of ether (the cryptocurrency of the Ethereum network) a user is willing to pay per unit of gas. The gas limit and gas price are used to calculate the total cost of the transaction, which is paid in ether. Miners are incentivized to process transactions by receiving a portion of the transaction fees in ether.

-Smart Contracts

Smart contracts are self-executing contracts with the terms of the agreement written into code. Smart contracts are stored on the Ethereum blockchain and can be executed by the EVM. They allow for the automation of complex agreements and transactions without the need for intermediaries.

Smart contracts are written in Solidity, a programming language specifically designed for the Ethereum network. Solidity allows developers to write complex programs, such as decentralized autonomous organizations (DAOs) and decentralized finance (DeFi) applications.

-Differences From Bitcoin

While Bitcoin and Ethereum are both decentralized blockchain networks, there are several key differences between the two.

1. First, Ethereum is designed as a platform for building decentralized applications, while Bitcoin is primarily a digital currency.

2. Additionally, while Bitcoin uses the Proof of Work algorithm to

validate transactions and add them to the blockchain, Ethereum uses the Proof of Stake algorithm.

3. Finally, while Bitcoin has a fixed supply of 21 million coins, there is no fixed limit on the number of ether that can be created on the Ethereum network.

In conclusion, Ethereum is a decentralized blockchain platform that allows for the creation and deployment of decentralized applications. Transactions on the Ethereum network are processed by miners, who are incentivized with transaction fees paid in ether.

Smart contracts allow for the automation of complex agreements and transactions without the need for intermediaries. While Ethereum shares many similarities with Bitcoin, there are key differences between the two networks, including Ethereum's focus on dApp development and its use of a different consensus algorithm.

Chapter 3

Tether (USDT)

Tether (USDT) is a stablecoin that has gained significant popularity among cryptocurrency traders and investors. Launched in 2014, it was one of the first stablecoins to hit the market, and has since become the most widely-used stablecoin, with a market capitalization of over $50 billion as of April 2023.

USDT is designed to maintain a stable value relative to the US dollar, with one USDT representing one US dollar in value. It achieves this stability by being backed by reserves of US dollars held in a bank account. For every USDT in circulation, there is supposed to be an equivalent amount of US dollars held in reserve.

The idea behind USDT is that it provides a way for traders to move funds between different cryptocurrency exchanges without having to convert their holdings into fiat currency. For example, a trader could buy USDT on one exchange using Bitcoin, and then transfer the USDT to another exchange where they could use it to buy other cryptocurrencies. This can be faster and cheaper than converting Bitcoin to fiat currency and then back into another cryptocurrency.

However, USDT has also been subject to controversy and criticism. One concern is that there may not be sufficient reserves of US dollars to back all of the USDT in circulation. Tether has claimed that all USDT is fully backed by reserves, but some critics have raised doubts about the transparency and legitimacy of Tether's reserves. Tether has faced legal challenges related to its reserves, including a settlement with the New York Attorney General's office in 2021.

Another criticism of USDT is that it may be used to manipulate the price of Bitcoin and other cryptocurrencies. Some traders have been accused of using USDT to artificially inflate the price of Bitcoin by buying large amounts of USDT and then using it to buy Bitcoin, creating the appearance of high demand for Bitcoin.

Despite these concerns, USDT remains a popular stablecoin in the cryptocurrency world. Its ability to maintain a stable value relative to the US dollar makes it a useful tool for traders and investors, and its widespread adoption means that it is easily accessible on most cryptocurrency exchanges.

However, it is important for users to be aware of the potential risks and controversies associated with USDT, and to make informed decisions when using it.

Chapter 4

BNB (BNB)

BNB (BNB) is the native cryptocurrency of the Binance exchange, one of the largest and most popular cryptocurrency exchanges in the world. Binance launched BNB in 2017 as part of its initial coin offering (ICO), and it has since become a major player in the cryptocurrency market, with a market capitalization of over $100 billion as of April 2023.

One of the main uses of BNB is to pay for trading fees on the Binance exchange. When traders use BNB to pay for fees, they receive a discount of up to 25% on the fees they would otherwise pay in Bitcoin or other cryptocurrencies. This makes BNB an attractive option for frequent traders who want to save money on fees.

In addition to its use as a fee payment option, BNB has also been used as a fundraising tool for blockchain projects through Binance Launchpad, a platform for hosting token sales. Projects that are selected for Launchpad can raise funds by selling their tokens for BNB. This has helped to fuel the growth of the Binance ecosystem, as successful projects are likely to attract new users and increase the trading volume on the exchange.

Another key feature of BNB is its use in the Binance Smart Chain (BSC), a blockchain platform that was launched by Binance in 2020. BNB is used as the primary fuel for transactions on the BSC, meaning that users must hold and use BNB to pay for transaction fees on the BSC. This has helped to drive demand for BNB and increase its value.

BNB also has other uses within the Binance ecosystem, such as being used to purchase virtual gifts on the Binance NFT marketplace and as collateral for borrowing on the Binance lending platform.

Despite its popularity and usefulness, BNB has not been without controversy. In 2021, the UK Financial Conduct Authority (FCA) issued a warning against Binance, citing concerns about its operations in the UK and the use of BNB as a fundraising tool. This led to a temporary dip in the value of BNB, but it has since recovered and continued to grow in value.

Overall, BNB has become an important cryptocurrency in the world of trading and blockchain projects, with a strong presence in the Binance ecosystem. Its utility and popularity suggest that it will continue to play an important role in the cryptocurrency market for years to come.

Chapter 5

USD Coin (USDC)

USD Coin (USDC) is a stablecoin that is pegged to the US dollar, with one USDC representing one US dollar in value. It was launched in 2018 as a collaboration between Circle and Coinbase, two of the largest cryptocurrency companies in the world, and has since become one of the most widely-used stablecoins, with a market capitalization of over $40 billion as of April 2023.

Like other stablecoins, USDC is designed to provide a stable and predictable value for traders and investors. It achieves this stability by being fully backed by US dollars held in a bank account. For every USDC in circulation, there is supposed to be an equivalent amount of US dollars held in reserve.

USDC is also designed to be transparent and auditable, with regular audits conducted by third-party accounting firms to ensure that the reserves match the number of USDC in circulation. This level of transparency and accountability has helped to build trust among users and increase the adoption of USDC.

One of the key features of USDC is its integration with a wide range of cryptocurrency exchanges and platforms. It is available on most major exchanges and is used as a trading pair for a variety of cryptocurrencies, making it a versatile and useful tool for traders.

USDC is also used in decentralized finance (DeFi) applications, where it can be used to provide liquidity for lending and borrowing protocols, or as collateral for borrowing other cryptocurrencies. Its stability and widespread adoption make it a popular choice for these applications, as it provides a predictable value that can be used to mitigate price volatility in other cryptocurrencies.

In addition to its use in trading and DeFi, USDC is also used for payments and remittances. It can be sent and received quickly and easily, with low transaction fees, making it an attractive option for cross-border transactions and other use cases where traditional payment methods may be slow or expensive.

Overall, USDC has become a key player in the stablecoin market, offering a stable and transparent option for traders and investors, as well as a useful tool for DeFi applications and payments. Its popularity and wide adoption suggest that it will continue to play an important role in the cryptocurrency world for years to come.

Chapter 6

XRP (XRP)

In the world of cryptocurrencies, XRP (XRP) has emerged as a game-changer for global payments. XRP is a digital currency that was created by Ripple Labs, a San Francisco-based fintech company, in 2012. Since then, XRP has grown to become one of the most popular and widely used cryptocurrencies in the world.

One of the key features of XRP is its speed of transaction processing. Unlike other cryptocurrencies that take minutes or even hours to confirm a transaction, XRP can settle transactions in just a few seconds. This makes XRP an ideal choice for cross-border payments, where speed and efficiency are crucial.

Another advantage of XRP is its low transaction fees. Compared to other cryptocurrencies like Bitcoin and Ethereum, which have high transaction fees due to the high demand and limited supply of block space, XRP has a negligible transaction fee. This makes XRP an attractive option for micropayments and other low-value transactions.

In addition to its speed and low fees, XRP also has the backing of major financial institutions. Ripple Labs has partnered with some of the biggest banks and payment providers in the world, including Santander, American Express, and Standard Chartered, to use XRP for cross-border payments. These partnerships have given XRP a level of legitimacy and acceptance in the financial industry that other cryptocurrencies have yet to achieve.

Despite its many advantages, XRP has also faced its fair share of challenges. In late 2020, the US Securities and Exchange Commission (SEC) filed a lawsuit against Ripple Labs, alleging that XRP was an unregistered security. This led to a sharp drop in the price of XRP and caused many exchanges to delist it from their platforms. The lawsuit is still ongoing, and its outcome could have significant implications for the future of XRP and the broader cryptocurrency industry.

Despite the challenges, the future of XRP looks bright. As the world becomes increasingly interconnected and the demand for fast and efficient cross-border payments grows, XRP is well-positioned to become the go-to cryptocurrency for global transactions. Its speed, low fees, and institutional backing make it a compelling choice for businesses and individuals alike.

In conclusion, XRP is a cryptocurrency that has the potential to revolutionize the way we make cross-border payments. With its speed, low fees, and institutional backing, XRP is well-positioned to become a major player in the global payments industry. While there are still challenges to overcome, the future of XRP looks bright and full of possibilities.

Chapter 7

Cardano (ADA)

Cardano (ADA) is a third-generation blockchain platform that aims to provide a more secure, sustainable, and scalable infrastructure for decentralized applications and smart contracts. Launched in 2017, Cardano was created by a team of academics, developers, and engineers led by Charles Hoskinson, one of the co-founders of Ethereum.

One of the key features of Cardano is its Proof of Stake (PoS) consensus mechanism, which enables faster transaction processing and lower energy consumption compared to the Proof of Work (PoW) mechanism used by Bitcoin and many other cryptocurrencies. Cardano's PoS mechanism is called Ouroboros, and it uses a unique algorithm to randomly select validators who verify and confirm transactions on the network.

Another important aspect of Cardano is its focus on research and peer review. The development of Cardano is guided by a scientific approach, with a team of researchers and academics constantly studying and refining the protocol to ensure its security, scalability, and sustainability.

Cardano also has a strong community of developers and enthusiasts who contribute to the project and help to build a thriving ecosystem of decentralized applications and services.

Cardano's native cryptocurrency, ADA, is used as a medium of exchange and a store of value on the network. Like Bitcoin and other cryptocurrencies, ADA can be used for peer-to-peer transactions and can be traded on cryptocurrency exchanges. However, Cardano also enables the creation of smart contracts and decentralized applications (dApps) that can be used for a variety of purposes, such as identity verification, supply chain management, and financial services.

One of the advantages of Cardano is its modular design, which allows for easy upgrades and improvements to the protocol without disrupting the entire network. Cardano is divided into two layers: the Cardano Settlement Layer (CSL) and the Cardano Computation Layer (CCL).

The CSL handles transactions and the distribution of ADA, while the CCL handles smart contracts and daApps. This separation of functions makes Cardano more flexible and adaptable to changing market conditions and user needs.

While Cardano is still relatively new and faces competition from other blockchain platforms, its unique features and scientific approach have made it an attractive option for developers and investors. Cardano has already seen significant growth in terms of market capitalization and adoption, and its potential for further growth and innovation is high.

In conclusion, Cardano is a third-generation blockchain platform that combines scientific rigor, modular design, and a focus on sustainability to provide a more secure, scalable, and flexible infrastructure for decentralized applications and smart contracts. With its PoS consensus mechanism, strong community, and commitment to research and development, Cardano is poised to become a major player in the blockchain industry and a key driver of innovation in the years to come.

Chapter 8

Dogecoin (DOGE)

Dogecoin is a decentralized, peer-to-peer cryptocurrency that was created in December 2013 by software developers Billy Markus and Jackson Palmer. The cryptocurrency was originally created as a joke, based on the popular "Doge" meme, which features a Shiba Inu dog with broken English captions. Despite its origins as a joke, Dogecoin has become a popular and valuable cryptocurrency, with a market capitalization of over $40 billion as of April 2023.

Dogecoin is based on the same code as Litecoin, a cryptocurrency that was created in 2011. It uses the Scrypt algorithm for mining, which is a memory-hard algorithm that is designed to be resistant to ASIC mining. Dogecoin has a block time of one minute, and a total supply of 129 billion coins, with new coins being created through mining rewards.

Dogecoin transactions are processed on a decentralized network, which is secured by a distributed network of miners. Transactions are validated through a POW consensus mechanism, which requires miners to solve complex mathematical problems in order to validate transactions and earn rewards.

-Advantages and Disadvantages

One of the main advantages of Dogecoin is its strong community and active development team. Dogecoin has a large and passionate community of users, who are active on social media and frequently use the cryptocurrency for charitable causes and community projects. Additionally, the Dogecoin development team has continued to update and improve the cryptocurrency over the years, with recent upgrades including the adoption of the AuxPoW (Auxiliary Proof of Work) algorithm, which allows Dogecoin miners to merge mine with Litecoin miners.

However, one of the disadvantages of Dogecoin is its lack of technical innovation. Unlike other cryptocurrencies, such as Bitcoin and Ethereum, which have introduced new and innovative features such as smart contracts and decentralized applications, Dogecoin has remained relatively unchanged since its creation in 2013. Additionally, Dogecoin's reliance on PoW mining has raised concerns about the environmental impact of the cryptocurrency, as mining requires a significant amount of energy and resources.

-Use Cases

Dogecoin is primarily used as a means of exchange and store of value, similar to other cryptocurrencies such as Bitcoin and Litecoin. However, Dogecoin's strong community and meme culture have also led to the creation of unique use cases, such as the "Doge4Water" campaign, which raised over $50,000 in Dogecoin to fund clean water initiatives in developing countries. Additionally, Dogecoin has been used to tip content creators on social media platforms such as Reddit and Twitter, as well as for charitable causes and community projects.

Dogecoin is a unique and popular cryptocurrency that has gained a large following thanks to its strong community and meme culture. While it may not have the technical innovation of other cryptocurrencies, Dogecoin's active development team and passionate community have helped it remain a popular and valuable asset in the cryptocurrency market.

However, as with any investment, it is important to understand the risks and potential drawbacks of investing in Dogecoin, and to carefully consider your own financial situation and investment goals before making any decisions.

Chapter 9

Polygon (MATIC)

Polygon (MATIC) is a layer 2 scaling solution for Ethereum, designed to address the network's high gas fees and slow transaction processing times. It aims to provide faster and cheaper transactions while maintaining the security and decentralization of Ethereum.

Polygon was originally founded as Matic Network in 2017 by Jaynti Kanani, Sandeep Nailwal, and Anurag Arjun. The team's goal was to build a layer 2 scaling solution for Ethereum that would provide a better user experience, reduce congestion, and make dApps more accessible. In February 2021, the Matic Network rebranded as Polygon to reflect its expanding scope beyond just a scaling solution for Ethereum.

Polygon's architecture is built on top of Ethereum and allows for interoperability with other blockchain networks. It is an open-source, modular framework that offers several components, including Polygon software development kit (SDK), Polygon POS Chain, Polygon AMM, Polygon PoS Bridge, and Polygon Plasma.

The Polygon SDK provides developers with tools to build dApps that can be deployed on the Polygon network. It supports Ethereum Virtual Machine (EVM) and Web3.js, making it easy for developers to migrate their existing Ethereum dApps to Polygon. The Polygon POS Chain is the main component of Polygon's architecture and serves as a layer 2 scaling solution for Ethereum. It uses a Proof of Stake (PoS) consensus mechanism to validate transactions, reducing the energy consumption required for mining on the Ethereum network.

Polygon AMM (Automated Market Maker) is a decentralized exchange (DEX) that allows users to trade cryptocurrencies in a trustless and permissionless manner. It uses an algorithm to determine the prices of assets and provides liquidity through automated trading pools. Polygon PoS Bridge enables seamless transfers of assets between Ethereum and Polygon networks.

The Polygon Plasma component is a scaling solution for dApps that require high throughput and low latency. It uses a sidechain construction to facilitate off-chain transactions, reducing congestion on the Ethereum network. Polygon Plasma supports Ethereum smart contracts and allows developers to build scalable and secure dApps.

Polygon's native token, MATIC, is used as a utility token to pay for transactions and fees on the network. It can also be staked to participate in network validation and earn rewards. In addition to staking, MATIC can be used for governance on the Polygon network, allowing token holders to vote on proposals and influence network decisions.

Polygon has gained significant attention and adoption in the blockchain space, with several high-profile partnerships and integrations with projects such as Aave, Chainlink, and Decentraland. It has also attracted several notable investors, including Mark Cuban, who announced in May 2021 that he had invested in the project.

In conclusion, Polygon (MATIC) has emerged as a promising layer 2 scaling solution for Ethereum, offering faster and cheaper transactions without sacrificing the security and decentralization of the network. With a growing ecosystem of dApps, developers, and investors, Polygon is poised to play a significant role in the future of blockchain technology.

Chapter 10

Solana (SOL)

Solana (SOL) is a high-performance blockchain that has been gaining traction in the cryptocurrency world due to its impressive speed and low transaction fees. Built by a team of seasoned blockchain engineers, Solana has quickly become one of the most exciting blockchain projects in the space.

The Solana blockchain was created to address the scalability issues that many other blockchains, such as Ethereum, have struggled with. Solana's unique architecture allows it to process up to 65,000 transactions per second, making it one of the fastest blockchains in the world. This is accomplished through the use of a novel consensus mechanism called Proof of History (PoH) and a network of parallel blockchains called "shards."

Proof of History is a mechanism that allows nodes on the Solana network to verify the order of transactions without having to process them. This significantly reduces the amount of time it takes for a transaction to be confirmed, as nodes no longer have to wait for other nodes to process the transaction before verifying its order. By using Proof of History, Solana is able to achieve high transaction throughput while maintaining a high level of security and decentralization.

In addition to Proof of History, Solana also uses a network of parallel blockchains called shards to further increase its transaction throughput. Each shard is capable of processing transactions independently, allowing for more transactions to be processed simultaneously. Sharding is a common technique used in other blockchain projects, but Solana's implementation is unique in that it allows shards to communicate with each other seamlessly, ensuring that the network remains cohesive and secure.

Solana's speed and scalability make it an ideal blockchain for decentralized applications (dApps) and other use cases that require fast and inexpensive transactions. Solana's low transaction fees, which are currently around $0.0001 per transaction, make it one of the most affordable blockchains to use. This has led to a growing number of projects building on the Solana blockchain, including some high-profile projects like Serum, Mango Markets, and Raydium.

The Solana team has also been actively working on expanding the capabilities of the Solana ecosystem. In addition to building out the core blockchain infrastructure, the Solana team has developed a number of tools and services to help developers build and deploy applications on the Solana network. These include a software development kit (SDK), a wallet, and a decentralized exchange (DEX).

The future of Solana looks promising, as the project continues to gain traction and attract new users and developers to its ecosystem. With its impressive speed and low transaction fees, Solana has the potential to become a major player in the blockchain space and drive innovation in decentralized finance (DeFi), gaming, and other areas of the decentralized web.

Chapter 11

Polkadot (DOT)

Polkadot (DOT) is a next-generation blockchain protocol that aims to address the issue of interoperability between different blockchains. Developed by Gavin Wood, one of the co-founders of Ethereum, Polkadot is designed to allow for the seamless exchange of data and assets between different blockchain networks.

At its core, Polkadot is a multi-chain network that allows different blockchains to communicate with each other using a common language. This is accomplished through the use of a relay chain, which acts as the main hub for the Polkadot network, and a series of parachains, which are specialized blockchains that can be tailored to specific use cases.

The relay chain is responsible for maintaining the security and consensus of the entire Polkadot network, while the parachains can be customized to support a variety of different applications and use cases. This modular design allows for greater flexibility and scalability, as new parachains can be added to the network as needed without affecting the overall performance or security of the network.

One of the key advantages of Polkadot is its ability to facilitate cross-chain communication and interoperability. This is achieved through the use of a messaging protocol called the Polkadot Cross-Chain Message Passing (XCMP) protocol. The XCMP protocol allows different parachains to communicate with each other and share data and assets in a secure and decentralized manner.

Polkadot's focus on interoperability has made it a popular choice for developers and projects looking to build decentralized applications (dApps) and other blockchain-based solutions. The Polkadot ecosystem has already attracted a number of high-profile projects, including Acala, Moonbeam, and Chainlink, all of which are building on the Polkadot network.

Another unique feature of Polkadot is its governance mechanism. Polkadot is designed to be a fully decentralized and community-driven network, with decisions about the future development and direction of the network made through a process of on-chain governance. This allows stakeholders to vote on proposals and changes to the network, ensuring that the community has a say in the evolution of the platform.

The future of Polkadot looks bright, as the project continues to gain momentum and attract new developers and users to its ecosystem. With its focus on interoperability and modularity, Polkadot has the potential to become a key player in the blockchain space, enabling new levels of innovation and collaboration between different blockchain networks.

As the world becomes more decentralized, the need for interoperability and collaboration between different blockchain networks will only continue to grow, and Polkadot is well-positioned to meet this need.

Chapter 12

Binance USD (BUSD)

Binance USD (BUSD) is a stablecoin that is pegged to the value of the U.S. dollar. Stablecoins like BUSD are designed to provide the benefits of cryptocurrencies, such as fast transaction times and low fees, while also maintaining a stable value that is not subject to the same price volatility as other cryptocurrencies like Bitcoin and Ethereum.

Stablecoins are becoming an increasingly popular option for cryptocurrency traders and investors, as they provide a way to move funds quickly and easily between different cryptocurrency exchanges without having to worry about fluctuations in value. They also offer a way to hedge against market volatility, as stablecoins can be exchanged for fiat currencies like the U.S. dollar at a 1:1 ratio.

BUSD was created by Binance, one of the largest cryptocurrency exchanges in the world. The stablecoin was launched in September 2019 and is now available on a number of different exchanges, including Binance, Coinbase, and Gemini. One of the key benefits of BUSD is its transparency and regulatory compliance. Unlike some other stablecoins that have faced questions about their reserves and backing, BUSD is fully backed by U.S. dollars held in FDIC-insured bank accounts. This provides users with peace of mind, as they can be confident that their BUSD tokens are backed by actual dollars held in secure and regulated institutions.

BUSD also offers fast transaction times and low fees, making it an attractive option for cryptocurrency traders and investors. Transactions on the Binance Smart Chain, which supports BUSD, can be completed in just a few seconds, and fees are typically much lower than those associated with other cryptocurrencies. Another advantage of BUSD is its integration with the Binance ecosystem. Binance offers a wide range of cryptocurrency trading and investment options, and BUSD can be used to trade on the Binance exchange or to participate in other Binance-related products and services.

Looking to the future, stablecoins like BUSD are likely to play an increasingly important role in the cryptocurrency landscape. As more individuals and institutions seek to enter the crypto market, the need for stable and secure options for buying, selling, and storing cryptocurrency will only continue to grow. With its strong regulatory compliance, transparency, and integration with the Binance ecosystem, BUSD is well-positioned to meet this growing demand for stable and reliable cryptocurrency options.

Chapter 13

Litecoin (LTC)

Litecoin (LTC) is a peer-to-peer cryptocurrency that was created in 2011 by Charlie Lee, a former Google engineer. Like Bitcoin, Litecoin is based on a decentralized, open-source protocol that enables fast, secure, and low-cost transactions without the need for intermediaries such as banks or payment processors.

One of the key features of Litecoin is its faster block generation time compared to Bitcoin. While Bitcoin blocks are generated every 10 minutes, Litecoin blocks are generated every 2.5 minutes, which means transactions can be confirmed and settled much faster on the Litecoin network. This makes Litecoin a more practical option for everyday transactions and micropayments. Another advantage of Litecoin is its lower transaction fees compared to Bitcoin. While Bitcoin fees can sometimes be high due to network congestion, Litecoin fees are usually much lower, making it an attractive option for people who want to avoid high fees and slow transaction times.

Litecoin is often referred to as the digital silver to Bitcoin's digital gold, due to its similarities to Bitcoin and its focus on being a practical, everyday cryptocurrency. Litecoin has a fixed maximum supply of 84 million coins, which is four times the maximum supply of Bitcoin. This means that Litecoin has a lower value per coin, but it also means that it has a greater potential for wider adoption and usage.

In addition to its practicality and low fees, Litecoin also has a strong community of developers and enthusiasts who contribute to its development and adoption. Litecoin has been around for over a decade and has withstood the test of time, making it a reliable and trusted cryptocurrency.

While Litecoin faces competition from other cryptocurrencies, it has a loyal following and a solid track record. Litecoin has been used for a variety of purposes, from everyday transactions to fundraising for charitable causes. Its fast transaction times, low fees, and strong community make it a promising option for people who want a practical and reliable cryptocurrency for their everyday needs.

In conclusion, Litecoin is a peer-to-peer cryptocurrency that was created to provide a faster, more practical alternative to Bitcoin. With its faster block generation time, lower transaction fees, and strong community, Litecoin has emerged as a reliable and trusted cryptocurrency that has the potential for wider adoption and usage. While there are challenges and competition in the cryptocurrency market, Litecoin's track record and loyal following make it a promising option for the future.

Chapter 14

Shiba Inu (SHIB)

Shiba Inu (SHIB) is a decentralized, peer-to-peer cryptocurrency that was created in August 2020. It is an ERC-20 token on the Ethereum blockchain, and was created as a "Dogecoin killer" in reference to the popular Dogecoin cryptocurrency. SHIB is part of a group of "meme coins" that have gained popularity due to their unique branding and strong online communities. SHIB is built on the Ethereum blockchain, which is a decentralized, open-source blockchain platform that allows developers to build decentralized applications (dApps) and smart contracts. As an ERC-20 token, SHIB can be stored in any Ethereum wallet that supports ERC-20 tokens, such as MyEtherWallet or MetaMask.

SHIB has a total supply of 1 quadrillion tokens, which is significantly larger than most other cryptocurrencies. The large supply is designed to keep the price of each individual token low, making it more accessible to a wider range of investors. SHIB transactions are processed on the Ethereum network, which is secured by a distributed network of miners.

-Advantages and Disadvantages

One of the main advantages of SHIB is its strong online community and active development team. SHIB has gained a large following on social media platforms such as Twitter and Reddit, with users frequently engaging in community projects and charitable causes. Additionally, the SHIB development team has continued to update and improve the cryptocurrency over time, with recent upgrades, including the launch of ShibaSwap, a decentralized exchange that allows users to trade SHIB and other cryptocurrencies.

However, one of the disadvantages of SHIB is its lack of technical innovation. While it shares some similarities with other cryptocurrencies, such as Ethereum and Bitcoin, SHIB does not introduce any new or innovative features. Additionally, the large supply of SHIB tokens has raised concerns about the potential for inflation and market manipulation, as large holders of the cryptocurrency could potentially manipulate the market by selling off their holdings.

-Use Cases

SHIB is primarily used as a means of exchange and store of value, similar to other cryptocurrencies. However, the strong online community and meme culture surrounding SHIB have led to the creation of unique use cases, such as the "WoofPaper" project, which aims to create a decentralized marketplace for buying and selling digital art using SHIB and other cryptocurrencies. Additionally, SHIB has been used to tip content creators on social media platforms such as Twitter and TikTok, as well as for charitable causes and community projects.

SHIB is a unique and popular cryptocurrency that has gained a large following thanks to its strong online community and unique branding. While it may not have the technical innovation of other cryptocurrencies, SHIB's active development team and passionate community have helped it remain a popular asset in the cryptocurrency market.

However, as with any investment, it is important to understand the risks and potential drawbacks of investing in SHIB, and to carefully consider your own financial situation and investment goals before making any decisions.

Chapter 15

TRONIX (TRX)

TRON (TRX) is a blockchain-based platform founded in September 2017 by Justin Sun, a young Chinese entrepreneur. The platform aims to decentralize the internet by creating a global, open-source, and decentralized content entertainment system. TRON aims to eliminate intermediaries and empower users to create, share, and own content without the interference of third parties. The platform provides a range of tools and services to support the development of decentralized applications (dApps) that leverage blockchain technology to deliver content and services directly to users.

TRON has a robust and active community, which has helped the platform to grow significantly since its inception. The platform's native cryptocurrency, TRONIX (TRX), is used to power transactions on the network, and it can be used to pay for content and services on the platform.

TRON has its own blockchain, which is based on the Delegated Proof of Stake (DPoS) consensus mechanism. This mechanism allows users to vote for super representatives who validate transactions on the network. The TRON blockchain is scalable, with a capacity to process up to 2,000 transactions per second.

The TRON platform supports the development of decentralized applications through its TRON Virtual Machine (TVM). The TVM is a lightweight, Turing-complete virtual machine that allows developers to build and deploy smart contracts on the TRON network. Smart contracts are self-executing contracts that can automate complex processes and transactions, enabling a range of decentralized services to be built on the TRON platform.

TRON also supports the creation of custom tokens through its TRC-20 token standard. This standard allows developers to create their own tokens on the TRON network, which can be used for a variety of purposes, such as fundraising or creating loyalty programs.

TRON's ecosystem includes a wide range of decentralized applications, including social media platforms, gaming applications, music streaming platforms, and more. Some of the most popular dApps on the TRON network include BitTorrent, TRONbet, and WINk. These dApps are powered by the TRON blockchain and provide users with a range of decentralized services.

TRON has also made significant progress in terms of partnerships and collaborations. The platform has formed partnerships with several companies in the entertainment industry, including the BitTorrent peer-to-peer file sharing network and the Opera web browser. These partnerships have helped to increase the visibility and adoption of the TRON platform.

In conclusion, TRON is a blockchain-based platform that aims to decentralize the internet by creating a global, open-source, and decentralized content entertainment system. The platform provides a range of tools and services to support the development of decentralized applications (dApps) that leverage blockchain technology to deliver content and services directly to users. With its dedicated team, strong community, and ambitious roadmap, TRON has the potential to become a major player in the blockchain industry in the years to come.

Chapter 16

Avalanche (AVAX)

Avalanche (AVAX) is a blockchain-based platform founded in 2018 by Emin Gün Sirer, a renowned computer scientist and blockchain researcher. The platform aims to provide fast, efficient, and highly scalable decentralized solutions to its users. Avalanche seeks to address the issues of slow transaction speeds and high fees that have plagued other blockchain networks, making it an attractive option for decentralized finance (DeFi) and other applications that require high throughput and low latency.

Avalanche is built on a consensus mechanism called Avalanche Consensus, which is a novel consensus mechanism that allows for extremely fast and secure transactions. Avalanche Consensus is a variation of the Proof of Stake (PoS) consensus mechanism, which allows users to participate in the validation of transactions on the network by staking their AVAX tokens.

Avalanche supports the creation of custom tokens through its Avalanche Standard Asset (ASA) protocol, which allows developers to create and issue their own tokens on the Avalanche network. These tokens can be used for a wide range of applications, including fundraising, reward programs, and gaming.

Avalanche also supports the development of decentralized applications (dApps) through its Avalanche-X program, which provides resources and support to developers building on the Avalanche network. Avalanche-X provides developers with access to tools, resources, and technical assistance to help them build and launch dApps on the Avalanche network.

One of the key features of Avalanche is its subnets architecture, which allows for the creation of independent blockchain networks that can operate within the Avalanche ecosystem. Subnets can have their own validators, consensus rules, and token economies, making it possible to create customized blockchain networks for specific use cases.

Another key feature of Avalanche is its interoperability with other blockchain networks. Avalanche is designed to be compatible with Ethereum, allowing developers to port their Ethereum-based dApps to the Avalanche network easily. Avalanche also supports the creation of bridges to other blockchain networks, which can facilitate the transfer of assets and data between different blockchain ecosystems.

In terms of governance, Avalanche is a decentralized network that is governed by its community of stakeholders. AVAX token holders have the right to vote on proposals related to network upgrades, network fees, and other important decisions affecting the network.

In conclusion, Avalanche is a high-performance blockchain network that is designed to provide fast, efficient, and highly scalable decentralized solutions to its users. With its novel consensus mechanism, support for custom tokens and dApps, interoperability with other blockchain networks, and strong governance model, Avalanche is well-positioned to become a major player in the blockchain industry in the years to come.

Chapter 17

Dai (DAI)

Dai (DAI) is a decentralized stablecoin that operates on the Ethereum blockchain. The stablecoin was launched in 2017 by MakerDAO, a decentralized autonomous organization that governs the creation and management of the Dai stablecoin.

Dai is designed to maintain a stable value of 1 USD, unlike other cryptocurrencies that experience volatile price fluctuations. Dai achieves price stability by being collateralized by other cryptocurrencies such as Ether (ETH), which are locked up in smart contracts on the Ethereum blockchain.

To generate Dai, users must first deposit their cryptocurrency holdings as collateral in the MakerDAO smart contract. The amount of Dai that can be generated depends on the value of the collateral deposited, as well as a collateralization ratio that is set by MakerDAO. The collateralization ratio represents the amount of collateral required to generate a certain amount of Dai, and it is set to ensure that the value of the collateral is always greater than the value of the generated Dai.

Once Dai is generated, it can be used as a stable store of value, a medium of exchange, or a unit of account. Dai is fully decentralized, meaning that it is not controlled by any single entity, and it can be transferred and traded freely on the Ethereum blockchain.

Dai has a number of advantages over traditional fiat-backed stablecoins. Firstly, Dai is completely decentralized, meaning that it is not subject to the same regulatory and censorship risks as fiat-backed stablecoins. Secondly, Dai can be generated and traded without the need for a central authority or trusted third party. This makes Dai more accessible to users who may not have access to traditional financial institutions.

In addition to its stability, Dai is also highly interoperable with other decentralized applications on the Ethereum blockchain. Dai can be used as a medium of exchange for a wide range of decentralized services, such as decentralized exchanges, lending platforms, and prediction markets.

To maintain the stability of the Dai stablecoin, MakerDAO regularly adjusts the collateralization ratio and issues new MKR tokens through a decentralized governance process. MKR token holders have the ability to vote on proposals related to the management of the Dai stablecoin, including changes to the collateralization ratio and the issuance of new MKR tokens.

In conclusion, Dai is a decentralized stablecoin that provides a stable store of value and medium of exchange on the Ethereum blockchain. With its collateralized model, interoperability with other decentralized applications, and decentralized governance model, Dai has emerged as a popular stablecoin in the decentralized finance (DeFi) ecosystem.

Chapter 18

Wrapped Bitcoin (WBTC)

Wrapped Bitcoin (WBTC) is an ERC-20 token that is pegged to the value of Bitcoin (BTC). It is a collaboration between several decentralized finance (DeFi) projects, including BitGo, Kyber Network, and Ren, that allows users to access the functionality of Bitcoin while taking advantage of the benefits of the Ethereum blockchain.

The concept behind WBTC is simple. BTC holders deposit their Bitcoin into a custodian, which then mints an equivalent amount of WBTC on the Ethereum blockchain. The WBTC tokens are then held in a smart contract and can be transferred and traded just like any other ERC-20 token.

WBTC provides a number of benefits over traditional Bitcoin. Firstly, it enables BTC holders to participate in the growing DeFi ecosystem. By holding WBTC, users can access a wide range of DeFi applications, such as decentralized exchanges, lending platforms, and yield farming protocols. These applications are not available to BTC holders because the Bitcoin blockchain is not designed to support smart contracts.

Secondly, WBTC is faster and cheaper to use than Bitcoin. Transactions on the Ethereum blockchain are generally faster and less expensive than transactions on the Bitcoin blockchain. This means that users can transfer and trade WBTC more quickly and at a lower cost than BTC.

WBTC is also more flexible than Bitcoin. By being an ERC-20 token, WBTC can be integrated with other Ethereum-based projects, such as wallets and payment systems. This enables users to use WBTC in a wider range of applications and use cases.

Finally, WBTC is more transparent than Bitcoin. The WBTC smart contract is fully audited and transparent, meaning that users can easily verify the amount of Bitcoin backing each WBTC token. This is important because it ensures that each WBTC token is fully backed by an equivalent amount of Bitcoin.

To ensure the transparency and security of the WBTC system, the token is governed by a consortium of decentralized organizations, including BitGo, Kyber Network, and Ren. These organizations are responsible for the management of the WBTC system, including the minting and burning of WBTC tokens.

In conclusion, Wrapped Bitcoin (WBTC) is a bridge between the Bitcoin and Ethereum ecosystems that allows Bitcoin holders to access the functionality of the Ethereum blockchain. By providing faster, cheaper, and more flexible access to Bitcoin, WBTC has emerged as a popular option for users looking to participate in the growing DeFi ecosystem.

Chapter 19

Chainlink (LINK)

Chainlink (LINK) is a decentralized oracle network that aims to connect smart contracts on the blockchain to real-world data and events. It was founded in 2017 by Sergey Nazarov and Steve Ellis, and is currently one of the most widely used oracle networks in the blockchain ecosystem.

Smart contracts are self-executing contracts that operate on the blockchain. They are designed to execute automatically when certain conditions are met, without the need for intermediaries or human intervention. However, smart contracts currently have limited access to external data and events, which limits their functionality.

This is where Chainlink comes in. The Chainlink network provides a secure and decentralized way to access off-chain data and events, such as stock prices, weather data, and sports scores, and make it available to smart contracts on the blockchain. This allows smart contracts to make decisions based on real-world data, and enables the creation of more complex and sophisticated decentralized applications.

Chainlink achieves this by using a decentralized network of oracles, which are trusted sources of data that provide information to smart contracts. Oracles are independent entities that are incentivized to provide accurate data, and they are selected based on their reputation, reliability, and performance.

The Chainlink network also uses a unique consensus mechanism called the "LINK token staking" system. In this system, node operators, who provide the necessary computing power and resources to run the Chainlink network, must stake a certain amount of LINK tokens. This creates an economic incentive for node operators to provide accurate data, as they risk losing their stake if they provide incorrect information.

One of the key benefits of Chainlink is its ability to provide secure and reliable data to smart contracts. This is achieved through the use of tamper-proof hardware security modules (HSMs) that are used to store private keys and sign data. This ensures that data cannot be manipulated or altered, and provides a high level of security for smart contract applications.

Chainlink has been adopted by a wide range of blockchain projects, including DeFi protocols, prediction markets, and gaming applications. It is widely regarded as one of the most important infrastructure projects in the blockchain ecosystem, and has gained a large following among developers and users alike.

In conclusion, Chainlink (LINK) is a decentralized oracle network that provides a secure and reliable way to connect smart contracts on the blockchain to real-world data and events. With its decentralized network of oracles, unique consensus mechanism, and tamper-proof security features, Chainlink has emerged as a key infrastructure project in the blockchain ecosystem.

Chapter 20

Unsus Sed Leo (Leo)

Leo is a decentralized cryptocurrency that was created in 2019. It is built on the Ethereum blockchain and is designed to provide fast and secure transactions. In this chapter, we will explore the history and technical aspects of Leo, as well as its current uses and potential for the future.

-The History of Leo:

Leo was created by Bitfinex, a cryptocurrency exchange that was founded in 2012. The goal of Leo was to create a cryptocurrency that would be used as a utility token for Bitfinex customers. Leo was launched as an initial exchange offering (IEO) on May 27, 2019, and was sold to investors for $1 each. The total supply of Leo was set at 1 billion tokens.

-Technical Aspects of Leo:

Leo is built on the Ethereum blockchain, which means that it is an ERC-

20 token. This makes it compatible with a wide range of wallets and other Ethereum-based applications. The token has a maximum supply of 1 billion, and the current circulating supply is around 991 million. Transactions on the Leo blockchain are processed using a consensus mechanism called delegated proof of stake (DPOS).

-Uses of Leo:

The primary use of Leo is as a utility token for Bitfinex customers. Holders of Leo tokens receive a discount on trading fees, as well as access to other features and benefits on the Bitfinex platform. Leo is also used as a means of payment for certain services on the platform, such as margin funding and lending.

Leo also has value as a tradable asset on cryptocurrency exchanges. The price of Leo is determined by supply and demand on these exchanges, and it can be traded against other cryptocurrencies, as well as fiat currencies like USD and EUR.

-Potential for the Future:

The future of Leo will depend on the adoption and success of the Bitfinex platform. If the exchange continues to grow and attract more customers, the demand for Leo as a utility token is likely to increase. Additionally, if more cryptocurrency exchanges start to accept Leo as a tradable asset, the value of the token could also increase.

There is also potential for Leo to be used in other applications outside of the Bitfinex platform. As an ERC-20 token, it can be integrated into a wide range of decentralized applications (dApps) and used for various purposes. This could include anything from gaming to social media platforms.

In conclusion Leo is a cryptocurrency that was created to serve a specific purpose – as a utility token for Bitfinex customers. However, it has also become a tradable asset on cryptocurrency exchanges and has potential for use in other applications. The success of Leo will depend on the success of Bitfinex and the adoption of the token by other platforms and applications.

Chapter 21

Cosmos (Atom)

Atom is a decentralized cryptocurrency that was created in 2017. It is built on the Tendermint blockchain and is designed to provide fast and secure transactions. In this chapter, we will explore the history and technical aspects of Atom, as well as its current uses and potential for the future.

-The History of Atom:

Atom was created by the team behind the Cosmos network, a decentralized network of interconnected blockchains. The goal of Atom was to provide a means of payment and governance for the Cosmos network. Atom was launched in an initial coin offering (ICO) on April 6, 2017, and was sold to investors for $0.10 each. The total supply of Atom was set at 237 million tokens.

-Technical Aspects of Atom:

Atom is built on the Tendermint blockchain, which is a proof-of-stake

(POS) consensus mechanism. This means that transactions on the Atom blockchain are processed by validators who stake their tokens as collateral. Validators are chosen through a voting process in which token holders participate.

Atom has a maximum supply of 236,754,877 tokens, with a current circulating supply of around 203 million. Transactions on the Atom blockchain are processed quickly and cheaply, making it a popular choice for micropayments and other small transactions.

-Uses of Atom:

The primary use of Atom is as a governance token for the Cosmos network. Token holders have the ability to vote on proposals and changes to the network, and can also stake their tokens to earn rewards. Atom is also used as a means of payment for certain services on the Cosmos network, such as hosting and storage.

Atom is also tradable on cryptocurrency exchanges, and its price is determined by supply and demand on these exchanges. It can be traded against other cryptocurrencies, as well as fiat currencies like USD and EUR.

-Potential for the Future:

The future of Atom will depend on the adoption and success of the Cosmos network. If the network continues to grow and attract more users and developers, the demand for Atom as a governance token and means of payment is likely to increase. Additionally, if more cryptocurrency exchanges start to accept Atom as a tradable asset, the value of the token could also increase.

There is also potential for Atom to be used in other applications outside of the Cosmos network. As a POS blockchain, it can be integrated into a wide range of decentralized applications (dApps) and used for various purposes. This could include anything from gaming to social media platforms.

In conclusion Atom is a cryptocurrency that was created to serve a specific purpose – as a governance token and means of payment for the Cosmos network. However, it has also become a tradable asset on cryptocurrency exchanges and has potential for use in other applications. The success of Atom will depend on the success of the Cosmos network and the adoption of the token by other platforms and applications.

Chapter 22

Uniswap (UNI)

Uniswap (UNI) is a decentralized cryptocurrency exchange (DEX) that allows users to trade cryptocurrencies without the need for intermediaries or a centralized order book. It was founded in 2018 by Hayden Adams, and is built on the Ethereum blockchain.

The Uniswap protocol is powered by smart contracts, which are self-executing contracts that operate on the blockchain. Unlike traditional centralized exchanges, which require users to deposit funds into a centralized wallet, Uniswap allows users to trade cryptocurrencies directly from their own wallets. This means that users always maintain control of their funds and are not subject to the security risks of a centralized exchange.

The Uniswap exchange uses an automated market maker (AMM) model, which uses mathematical formulas to determine the price of a cryptocurrency based on its supply and demand. This eliminates the need for a centralized order book and allows for instant trades at any time, without the need for matching buyers and sellers.

In the Uniswap AMM model, liquidity providers (LPs) provide pairs of cryptocurrencies to a liquidity pool, which is used to facilitate trades on the exchange. LPs earn a portion of the trading fees generated by the liquidity pool in proportion to their contribution. This incentivizes users to provide liquidity to the exchange, which helps to increase liquidity and reduce slippage.

Uniswap has also introduced its own native token, UNI, which was launched in September 2020. UNI is used to govern the Uniswap protocol and allows holders to participate in the decision-making process for the future development of the exchange. It is also used to incentivize users to provide liquidity to the exchange, by rewarding them with UNI tokens for their contributions.

Since its launch, Uniswap has become one of the most widely used DEXs in the cryptocurrency ecosystem, and has played a significant role in the growth of the decentralized finance (DeFi) movement. It has been adopted by a wide range of DeFi projects, and has facilitated billions of dollars in trading volume.

In conclusion, Uniswap (UNI) is a decentralized cryptocurrency exchange that uses an automated market maker model to facilitate trades without the need for intermediaries or a centralized order book. With its focus on user control and incentivized liquidity provision, Uniswap has emerged as one of the most important projects in the DeFi ecosystem.

Chapter 23

Monero (XMR)

Monero (XMR) is a decentralized, privacy-focused cryptocurrency that was launched in 2014. It is built on the principles of privacy, security, and fungibility, and aims to provide a secure and untraceable way to conduct transactions online.

One of the key features of Monero is its focus on privacy. Unlike other cryptocurrencies, such as Bitcoin, Monero uses a unique technology called "ring signatures" to obfuscate the sender and receiver of transactions, as well as the amount being transacted. This makes it very difficult to trace transactions back to their original source, ensuring a high level of privacy for Monero users.

In addition to ring signatures, Monero also uses stealth addresses, which allow users to generate multiple one-time use addresses for each transaction. This makes it even more difficult to trace transactions, as each transaction appears to be sent to a unique address.

Monero also has a dynamic block size, which means that the size of each block is adjusted automatically based on the amount of transactions being processed. This ensures that the Monero network can handle a large volume of transactions without becoming congested or slowing down.

Another important feature of Monero is its focus on fungibility. Fungibility refers to the ability of a currency or asset to be exchanged for another unit of the same currency or asset, without any difference in value. Monero ensures fungibility by ensuring that each unit of XMR is interchangeable with any other unit, regardless of its transaction history.

In terms of mining, Monero uses a Proof of Work (PoW) consensus algorithm, which is used to validate transactions and generate new XMR coins. However, unlike Bitcoin, Monero uses a unique mining algorithm called "RandomX," which is designed to be ASIC-resistant. This means that mining on Monero can be done using a regular computer or laptop, making it more accessible to a wider range of users.

Monero has been adopted by a wide range of users and businesses, and is often used for transactions that require a high level of privacy and security, such as online purchases and donations to charities or political campaigns.

In conclusion, Monero (XMR) is a decentralized, privacy-focused cryptocurrency that offers a high level of anonymity and fungibility. With its use of unique technologies such as ring signatures and stealth addresses, Monero has become one of the most widely used privacy-focused cryptocurrencies in the cryptocurrency ecosystem.

Chapter 24

OKB

OBK is a decentralized cryptocurrency that was created in 2018. It is built on the Blockchain of Knowledge platform and is designed to provide fast and secure transactions. In this chapter, we will explore the history and technical aspects of OBK, as well as its current uses and potential for the future.

-The History of OBK:

OBK was created by a team of developers who wanted to create a blockchain platform that could be used for knowledge sharing and collaboration. The goal of OBK was to create a decentralized platform that could be used by individuals and organizations to share knowledge and collaborate on projects. OBK was launched in an initial coin offering (ICO) on June 30, 2018, and was sold to investors for $0.10 each. The total supply of OBK was set at 500 million tokens.

-Technical Aspects of OBK:

OBK is built on the Blockchain of Knowledge platform, which is a decentralized knowledge-sharing platform. The platform uses a proof-of-stake (POS) consensus mechanism, which means that transactions on the OBK blockchain are processed by validators who stake their tokens as collateral. Validators are chosen through a voting process in which token holders participate.

OBK has a maximum supply of 500 million tokens, with a current circulating supply of around 450 million. Transactions on the OBK blockchain are processed quickly and cheaply, making it a popular choice for micropayments and other small transactions.

-Uses of OBK:

The primary use of OBK is as a means of payment for services on the Blockchain of Knowledge platform. OBK can be used to pay for access to knowledge-sharing tools and resources, as well as for collaboration and project management tools.

OBK is also tradable on cryptocurrency exchanges, and its price is determined by supply and demand on these exchanges. It can be traded against other cryptocurrencies, as well as fiat currencies like USD and EUR.

-Potential for the Future:

The future of OBK will depend on the adoption and success of the Blockchain of Knowledge platform. If the platform continues to grow and attract more users and organizations, the demand for OBK as a means of payment is likely to increase. Additionally, if more cryptocurrency exchanges start to accept OBK as a tradable asset, the value of the token could also increase.

There is also potential for OBK to be used in other knowledge-sharing and collaboration applications outside of the Blockchain of Knowledge platform. As a POS blockchain, it can be integrated into a wide range of decentralized applications (dApps) and used for various purposes.

In conclusion, OBK is a cryptocurrency that was created to serve a specific purpose – as a means of payment for services on the Blockchain of Knowledge platform. However, it has also become a tradable asset on cryptocurrency exchanges and has potential for use in other applications. The success of OBK will depend on the success of the Blockchain of Knowledge platform and the adoption of the token by other platforms and applications.

Chapter 25

Ethereum Classic (ETC)

Ethereum Classic (ETC) is a decentralized, open-source blockchain platform that was created in 2016 as a result of a hard fork from the original Ethereum (ETH) blockchain. The split occurred as a result of disagreements within the Ethereum community over the handling of a high-profile hacking incident.

Like Ethereum, Ethereum Classic allows developers to build decentralized applications (dapps) and smart contracts using a programming language called Solidity. However, unlike Ethereum, Ethereum Classic is designed to operate as a more decentralized and immutable blockchain platform, with a focus on maintaining the original principles of blockchain technology.

One of the key features of Ethereum Classic is its focus on immutability. This means that once a transaction has been recorded on the Ethereum Classic blockchain, it cannot be changed or reversed. This ensures that the integrity of the blockchain is maintained and that the transactions recorded on the blockchain are secure and transparent.

Ethereum Classic also uses a Proof of Work (PoW) consensus algorithm, similar to Bitcoin, which is used to validate transactions and add new blocks to the blockchain. This process is carried out by miners, who use specialized hardware to solve complex mathematical problems in order to validate transactions and earn ETC rewards.

Another important feature of Ethereum Classic is its focus on interoperability. This means that Ethereum Classic is designed to work with other blockchain platforms and to facilitate the transfer of assets between different blockchains. This is achieved through the use of cross-chain bridges and interoperability protocols, which allow different blockchain platforms to communicate with each other and to exchange assets.

Since its creation, Ethereum Classic has been adopted by a wide range of developers and businesses, and has been used to build a variety of decentralized applications and blockchain-based solutions. It has also been listed on a wide range of cryptocurrency exchanges, making it easily accessible to users around the world.

In conclusion, Ethereum Classic (ETC) is a decentralized, open-source blockchain platform that offers a focus on immutability, decentralization, and interoperability. With its use of Proof of Work consensus and a focus on maintaining the original principles of blockchain technology, Ethereum Classic has become a popular blockchain platform for developers and businesses alike.

Chapter 26

Toncoin (Ton)

Toncoin (TON) is a decentralized blockchain network designed to enable fast, secure, and scalable peer-to-peer transactions. It was developed by Telegram, a popular messaging app, in collaboration with a team of blockchain experts, and was set to launch in 2019. However, the launch was postponed due to regulatory challenges.

In this chapter, we will provide an overview of Toncoin, including its features, use cases, and potential benefits. We will also examine its technology, governance, and token economics.

-Technology

Toncoin is built on a new blockchain protocol called the Telegram Open Network (TON). The TON protocol uses a combination of proof-of-stake (PoS) and Byzantine fault tolerance (BFT) consensus algorithms to achieve fast and secure transactions. It also features a unique sharding mechanism that enables it to scale to handle millions of transactions per second.

The TON blockchain has several unique features that set it apart from other blockchain networks. For instance, it supports smart contracts written in multiple programming languages, including Solidity, C++, and Python. It also has a built-in anonymous messaging system that enables users to send messages that cannot be traced back to their identities.

-Governance

The Toncoin network is governed by a decentralized community of users who hold TON tokens. These token holders have the right to vote on network upgrades, protocol changes, and other important decisions. The governance structure is designed to be transparent and democratic, with all token holders having an equal say in the decision-making process.

-Token Economics

The TON token is the native cryptocurrency of the Toncoin network. It is used to pay transaction fees, incentivize node operators, and participate in network governance. The total supply of TON tokens is capped at 5 billion, with 50% allocated for initial distribution and the remaining 50% reserved for future use.

-Use Cases

Toncoin has several potential use cases, including:

1. Decentralized Finance (DeFi): Toncoin can be used as a means of exchange and store of value in decentralized financial applications such as lending, borrowing, and trading.

2. Secure Messaging: Toncoin's built-in anonymous messaging system can be used to send private messages that cannot be traced back to the sender's identity.

3. Gaming: Toncoin can be used as an in-game currency for decentralized gaming platforms, enabling players to earn rewards and trade items with each other.

4. Internet of Things (IoT): Toncoin can be used as a means of payment for IoT devices, enabling them to transact with each other without the need for intermediaries.

-Potential Benefits

Toncoin has several potential benefits, including:

1. Fast and Secure Transactions: Toncoin's unique combination of PoS and BFT consensus algorithms enables it to achieve fast and secure transactions.

2. Scalability: Toncoin's sharding mechanism enables it to scale to handle millions of transactions per second, making it suitable for high-volume applications.

3. Decentralization: Toncoin's decentralized governance structure ensures that no single entity can control the network, making it resistant to censorship and manipulation.

4. Transparency: Toncoin's transparent governance structure ensures that all decision-making is visible to the community,

In conclusion Toncoin is a promising blockchain network with several unique features and potential use cases. Its fast and secure transaction processing, scalability, and decentralized governance structure make it a strong contender in the blockchain space. However, regulatory challenges and competition from other blockchain networks remain significant obstacles to its widespread adoption.

Chapter 27

Stellar (XLM)

Stellar (XLM) is a blockchain-based decentralized platform that aims to simplify the process of exchanging assets and making payments across borders. It was launched in 2014 by Jed McCaleb, who also co-founded Ripple. Stellar's main focus is on enabling fast and affordable cross-border payments, as well as facilitating asset transfers of various types, including cryptocurrencies and fiat currencies. This chapter provides a comprehensive guide to Stellar, including its history, technology, use cases, and future prospects.

-History:

Stellar was created in 2014 as an open-source, nonprofit platform that aimed to improve the efficiency and affordability of cross-border payments. The project was initially launched as a fork of Ripple, with Jed McCaleb taking the lead in development. However, Stellar was designed to be more decentralized and community-driven than Ripple. The platform initially used its own cryptocurrency called Stellar Lumens

(XLM) as a means of facilitating transactions and incentivizing network participants. The XLM token was also used as a bridge currency to enable cross-currency transactions on the platform.

In 2015, the Stellar Development Foundation (SDF) was established to oversee the development and promotion of the Stellar platform. The SDF is a nonprofit organization that is funded by donations and grants, and it is responsible for maintaining the codebase, organizing community events, and fostering partnerships with other organizations.

-Technology:

Stellar uses a consensus algorithm called the Stellar Consensus Protocol (SCP) to validate transactions and maintain the integrity of the network. SCP is a federated Byzantine agreement (FBA) algorithm that allows network nodes to reach consensus without relying on a central authority. SCP is designed to be fast, scalable, and energy-efficient, making it well-suited for use cases that require high transaction throughput and low fees.

Stellar also has a unique feature called the Stellar Decentralized Exchange (SDEX), which allows users to trade assets directly on the Stellar network without having to go through a centralized exchange. The SDEX is a peer-to-peer trading platform that supports various types of assets, including cryptocurrencies, fiat currencies, and commodities. The SDEX is also integrated with the Stellar Wallet, which allows users to easily manage their assets and make trades directly from their wallets.

-Use Cases:

Stellar's main use case is facilitating cross-border payments, particularly in developing countries where traditional banking infrastructure is limited or expensive. Stellar's low transaction fees and fast settlement times make it an attractive alternative to traditional payment methods, such as wire transfers and remittance services. Stellar has already partnered with several organizations to facilitate cross-border payments, including IBM and the UN World Food Programme.

Stellar is also used for asset transfers, including cryptocurrencies and fiat currencies. The platform's low transaction fees and fast settlement times make it an attractive option for traders and investors who want to move assets quickly and inexpensively. The SDEX also enables users to trade a wide range of assets, including cryptocurrencies that are not listed on centralized exchanges.

-Future Prospects:

Stellar's future prospects look bright, as the platform continues to gain adoption and attract new partners. Stellar's focus on cross-border payments and asset transfers is an area that is ripe for disruption, and Stellar's fast and affordable platform is well-positioned to capture a significant share of this market. Stellar's partnerships with IBM and the UN World Food Programme demonstrate the platform's potential to make a real-world impact and improve the lives of people in developing countries.

In conclusion Stellar (XLM) is a blockchain-based decentralized platform that aims to simplify the process of exchanging assets and making payments across borders. Stellar's fast and affordable platform, combined with its focus on cross-border payments and asset transfers, make it an attractive option for traders, investors, and organizations. As Stellar

Chapter 28

Internet Computer (ICP)

Internet Computer (ICP) is a decentralized, blockchain-based platform that allows developers to build and deploy applications on a global, open network. It was launched in May 2021 by the DFINITY Foundation, a nonprofit organization that aims to create a more open, decentralized internet. Internet Computer aims to provide a new model for building and deploying applications that is more efficient, secure, and cost-effective than traditional cloud computing solutions. This chapter provides an in-depth guide to Internet Computer, including its technology, use cases, and future prospects.

-Technology:

Internet Computer is built on a new type of blockchain called the Internet Computer Protocol (ICP). The ICP blockchain is designed to be more scalable, efficient, and interoperable than other blockchain networks. It uses a novel consensus mechanism called Chain Key Technology, which enables the network to support thousands of independent blockchains, or "subnets," that can interact with each other seamlessly. The ICP blockchain also features a novel "subnet governance" system that allows network participants to propose and vote on changes to the network.

Internet Computer also features a new type of programming language called Motoko, which is specifically designed for developing applications on the ICP blockchain. Motoko is a functional programming language that is easy to learn and provides powerful tools for building decentralized applications. Motoko is designed to be compatible with other programming languages, which allows developers to build applications using a wide range of tools and libraries.

-Use Cases:

Internet Computer has a wide range of potential use cases, from decentralized finance (DeFi) and gaming to social media and e-commerce. Some of the most promising use cases for Internet Computer include:

1. Decentralized Finance (DeFi): Internet Computer provides a more efficient and cost-effective platform for building and deploying DeFi applications, such as decentralized exchanges, lending platforms, and stablecoins.

2. Gaming: Internet Computer provides a new model for building and deploying online games that is more secure, transparent, and decentralized than traditional gaming platforms.

3. Social Media: Internet Computer provides a more open and decentralized platform for building and deploying social media applications that respect user privacy and data ownership.

4. E-commerce: Internet Computer provides a more efficient and cost-effective platform for building and deploying e-commerce applications, such as online marketplaces and payment gateways.

-Future Prospects:

Internet Computer has a bright future ahead, as the platform continues to gain adoption and attract new developers and users. Internet Computer's focus on efficiency, scalability, and interoperability makes it well-suited for a wide range of use cases, from DeFi and gaming to social media and e-commerce. Internet Computer's novel Chain Key Technology and subnet governance system also provide a more flexible and adaptable platform for developers to build and deploy applications. As the platform continues to mature and attract new partners and users, it has the potential to become a major player in the decentralized application (dApp) space.

In conclusion, Internet Computer (ICP) is a decentralized, blockchain-based platform that provides a new model for building and deploying applications on a global, open network. Internet Computer's focus on efficiency, scalability, and interoperability makes it well-suited for a wide range of use cases, from DeFi and gaming to social media and e-commerce. As the platform continues to mature and attract new partners and users, it has the potential to become a major player in the decentralized application (dApp) space.

Chapter 29

Bitcoin Cash (BCH)

Bitcoin Cash (BCH) is a decentralized digital currency that was created in 2017 as a result of a hard fork of the Bitcoin (BTC) blockchain. A hard fork is a significant change to a blockchain's protocol that creates a new blockchain with separate rules and features from the original blockchain. The hard fork was created in response to the scaling debate within the Bitcoin community, which involved disagreement on how to increase the network's capacity to handle more transactions. Bitcoin Cash was created with the intention of addressing the scaling issues that Bitcoin was facing.

Bitcoin Cash has a similar design and architecture to Bitcoin, as it is based on the same open-source code and uses a consensus mechanism based on proof-of-work mining. However, Bitcoin Cash has several distinct features that differentiate it from Bitcoin, including a larger block size limit of 32 MB (compared to Bitcoin's 1 MB limit) and a different difficulty adjustment algorithm.

The larger block size limit enables Bitcoin Cash to handle more transactions per second than Bitcoin. Additionally, Bitcoin Cash has lower transaction fees and faster confirmation times than Bitcoin due to its larger block size limit.

Bitcoin Cash is often seen as a currency that is more suitable for everyday use compared to Bitcoin. It is accepted by a growing number of merchants and can be used for online purchases, remittances, and peer-to-peer transactions.

Overall, Bitcoin Cash aims to provide a fast, low-cost, and reliable cryptocurrency that can be used for day-to-day transactions. While it shares similarities with Bitcoin, it has a distinct identity and set of features that make it an attractive alternative for individuals and businesses alike.

Chapter 30

TrueUSD (TUSD)

TrueUSD (TUSD) is a stablecoin that was launched in 2018 by TrustToken, a blockchain technology company based in San Francisco. TrueUSD is designed to be a stable and reliable alternative to other cryptocurrencies, which are known for their volatility and price fluctuations. TrueUSD is pegged to the US dollar at a 1:1 ratio, which means that one TUSD token is always equal in value to one US dollar. This chapter provides an in-depth guide to TrueUSD, including its technology, use cases, and future prospects.

-Technology:

TrueUSD is built on the Ethereum blockchain, which provides a secure and decentralized platform for issuing and transacting with the stablecoin. TrueUSD is an ERC-20 token, which means that it is compatible with a wide range of wallets and exchanges that support the Ethereum network. TrueUSD's stability is ensured through a collateralization process, where each TUSD token is backed by an equivalent amount of US dollars held in reserve by TrustToken. This means that for every TUSD token in circulation, there is an equivalent amount of US dollars held in reserve, which ensures the stability of the stablecoin.

-Use Cases:

TrueUSD has a wide range of potential use cases, from cross-border payments and remittances to e-commerce and peer-to-peer transactions. Some of the most promising use cases for TrueUSD include:

1. Cross-border Payments: TrueUSD provides a more efficient and cost-effective solution for cross-border payments and remittances, as it eliminates the need for intermediaries and reduces transaction fees.

2. E-commerce: TrueUSD provides a stable and reliable payment solution for online merchants and consumers, as it eliminates the risks associated with currency fluctuations and chargebacks.

3. Peer-to-Peer Transactions: TrueUSD provides a secure and fast solution for peer-to-peer transactions, as it enables users to send and receive payments without the need for intermediaries or banks.

4. Savings and Investments: TrueUSD provides a stable and secure asset for investors and savers, as it offers a reliable store of value that is not subject to the volatility of other cryptocurrencies.

-Future Prospects:

TrueUSD has a bright future ahead, as the stablecoin continues to gain adoption and attract new users and investors. TrueUSD's focus on stability and reliability makes it well-suited for a wide range of use cases, from cross-border payments and e-commerce to savings and investments. TrueUSD's collateralization process and transparent auditing practices also provide a high level of trust and security for users and investors. As the stablecoin continues to mature and gain wider adoption, it has the potential to become a major player in the future of finance.

In conclusion TrueUSD (TUSD) is a stablecoin that provides a stable and reliable alternative to other cryptocurrencies. TrueUSD is built on the Ethereum blockchain and is collateralized by US dollars held in reserve by TrustToken, which ensures the stability of the stablecoin. TrueUSD has a wide range of potential use cases, from cross-border payments and e-commerce to savings and investments. As the stablecoin continues to gain adoption and attract new users and investors, it has the potential to become a major player in the future of finance.

Chapter 31

Filecoin (FIL)

Filecoin is a decentralized storage network that allows users to store, retrieve, and share data in a secure and efficient manner. The project was launched in 2017 by Protocol Labs, a research, development, and deployment lab focused on the creation of peer-to-peer protocols and applications. The Filecoin network is powered by the InterPlanetary File System (IPFS), a peer-to-peer protocol for storing and sharing hypermedia in a distributed file system. In this chapter, we will explore the architecture, components, and applications of Filecoin.

-Architecture

Filecoin uses a unique consensus mechanism called Proof of Replication (PoRep) to incentivize users to store and distribute data on the network. PoRep is a verifiable process in which a miner creates a unique copy of a file, known as a "sector", and then proves that they have stored that copy by providing a cryptographic proof to the network. This process ensures that data is replicated across multiple nodes in the network, making it highly resistant to censorship and data loss.

Filecoin also uses a Proof of Spacetime (PoSt) consensus mechanism to ensure that miners are storing data for the full duration of their storage contracts. PoSt requires miners to provide cryptographic proof that they are still storing the data at regular intervals, which helps to prevent them from abandoning their storage commitments.

-Components

Filecoin has several key components that enable it to function as a decentralized storage network. These include:

1. The Filecoin blockchain: This is the underlying technology that powers the Filecoin network. It uses a modified version of the Bitcoin consensus algorithm to validate transactions and maintain the integrity of the network.

2. The Filecoin protocol: This is the set of rules and guidelines that govern how data is stored, retrieved, and shared on the network. It includes the PoRep and PoSt consensus mechanisms, as well as rules for data encryption and retrieval.

3. The Filecoin miner: This is a software program that runs on a computer or server and participates in the storage and retrieval of data on the network. Miners earn Filecoin tokens for providing storage and processing power to the network.

4. The Filecoin wallet: This is a digital wallet that users can use to store and manage their Filecoin tokens. It allows users to send and receive tokens, view transaction history, and monitor their account balance.

-Applications

Filecoin has a wide range of applications in various industries, including:

1. Decentralized cloud storage: Filecoin can be used as a more secure and cost-effective alternative to centralized cloud storage providers like Amazon Web Services and Google Cloud.

Because data is stored across a decentralized network, it is less vulnerable to data breaches and downtime.

2. Content distribution: Filecoin can be used to store and distribute large files such as videos, music, and software. This can help content creators to distribute their work more efficiently and with greater control over access and usage.

3. Decentralized finance (DeFi): Filecoin can be used as collateral for DeFi lending and borrowing platforms. This allows users to borrow Filecoin tokens against their existing holdings, without the need for a central intermediary.

4. Data archiving: Filecoin can be used to store and preserve historical data, such as scientific research, cultural artifacts, and government records. This can help to ensure that valuable information is preserved for future generations.

In conclusion Filecoin is a decentralized storage network that offers a more secure and efficient alternative to centralized cloud storage providers. Its unique consensus mechanism and protocol ensure that data is replicated and stored across a decentralized network, making it highly resistant to censorship and data loss. Filecoin has a wide range of applications in various industries, including decentralized cloud storage, content distribution, DeFi, and data archiving. As the world becomes increasingly reliant on

Chapter 32

Flow (FLOW)

Flow is a blockchain platform designed to enable decentralized applications (dApps) and digital assets for mainstream audiences. The platform is built on a unique architecture that allows for high throughput, low latency, and low transaction fees, making it suitable for a wide range of use cases, including games, collectibles, and non-fungible tokens (NFTs).

One of the key features of Flow is its ability to handle large-scale applications with high transaction volume. The platform uses a sharding mechanism that divides the network into different nodes, each of which can process a subset of transactions in parallel. This allows Flow to achieve high throughput and low latency, even when handling large-scale applications.

Another important feature of Flow is its focus on usability and developer experience. The platform provides a range of tools and resources for developers to build and deploy dApps and digital assets on the network, including a user-friendly programming language called Cadence. Flow also provides a marketplace for users to discover and purchase dApps and digital assets, making it easy for mainstream audiences to participate in the blockchain ecosystem.

Flow has gained attention for its partnerships with leading companies and organizations in the entertainment industry. The platform has formed partnerships with top brands like the NBA, UFC, and Warner Music Group, which have used Flow to create digital collectibles and other fan experiences. These partnerships have helped to drive adoption of Flow and showcase its potential for mainstream audiences.

In terms of adoption, Flow has seen significant growth since its launch in 2020. The platform has a growing ecosystem of developers and users, with a range of applications and digital assets already built on the network. Flow has also received support from a number of leading blockchain investors and organizations, including Andreessen Horowitz and Coinbase Ventures.

In conclusion, Flow is a blockchain platform designed to enable decentralized applications and digital assets for mainstream audiences. Its focus on high throughput, low latency, and usability make it an attractive option for a wide range of use cases, including games, collectibles, and NFTs. As the blockchain industry continues to evolve, Flow is well-positioned to play an important role in shaping the future of decentralized applications and digital assets.

Chapter 33

Hedera (HBAR)

Hedera Hashgraph is a distributed ledger technology (DLT) platform that uses a unique consensus algorithm to achieve high transaction throughput, fast finality, and a high degree of security. Launched in 2018, Hedera is designed to provide a fast, secure, and scalable infrastructure for decentralized applications (dApps) and enterprise use cases.

The Hedera platform is built on a proprietary consensus algorithm called hashgraph, which uses a combination of gossip protocol and virtual voting to achieve consensus. Unlike other consensus algorithms used by blockchain platforms like Bitcoin and Ethereum, hashgraph can achieve high transaction throughput without sacrificing finality or security. With hashgraph, transactions can be finalized within seconds, and the network can support hundreds of thousands of transactions per second.

Hedera's native cryptocurrency is called HBAR, which is used to pay for transactions on the Hedera network and can be staked to participate in network governance decisions. HBAR has a fixed maximum supply of 50 billion tokens, with a circulating supply of around 8 billion tokens as of May 2023. HBAR has been listed on numerous cryptocurrency exchanges and can be used to pay for a variety of services on the Hedera platform.

One of the key features of Hedera is its support for smart contracts, which allows developers to build dApps on top of the Hedera network. Hedera's smart contract language is based on Solidity, the same language used by Ethereum, making it easier for developers to transition from Ethereum to Hedera. The Hedera platform also includes a range of development tools and resources to help developers build, test, and deploy dApps on the platform.

Another unique feature of the Hedera platform is its focus on enterprise adoption. Hedera is designed to meet the needs of businesses and institutions, with features like low transaction fees, high transaction throughput, and support for regulatory compliance. Hedera has partnerships with a number of major companies, including IBM, Google Cloud, and Tata Communications, who are using the platform to build enterprise-grade applications.

Overall, Hedera is a promising DLT platform that has the potential to become a major player in the blockchain and cryptocurrency space. With its innovative consensus algorithm, native cryptocurrency, support for smart contracts, and focus on enterprise adoption, Hedera is well-positioned to meet the needs of developers, businesses, and institutions in the years to come.

Chapter 34

Cronos (CRO)

Cronos (CRO) is a layer 2 solution for Ethereum that aims to provide a fast, scalable, and cost-effective infrastructure for decentralized applications (dApps) and other use cases. Launched in 2021, Cronos is built on top of the Cosmos Network and uses the Tendermint consensus algorithm to achieve consensus.

Cronos is designed to address the scalability and high transaction fees issues associated with the Ethereum network. By leveraging the Cosmos Network's interoperability capabilities, Cronos can support cross-chain interactions with other blockchain networks, making it possible for dApps and users to access a wider range of services and applications.

Cronos has its native cryptocurrency called CRO, which is used to pay for transactions on the network and can be staked to participate in network governance decisions. The maximum supply of CRO is 10 billion tokens, with a circulating supply of around 4.7 billion tokens as of May 2023. CRO is listed on numerous cryptocurrency exchanges and can be used to pay for various services and applications on the Cronos network.

One of the key features of Cronos is its support for the Ethereum Virtual Machine (EVM), which allows Ethereum-based dApps to run on the Cronos network without any modifications. This means that developers can easily port their Ethereum-based dApps to Cronos, taking advantage of its faster transaction speeds and lower fees while maintaining compatibility with the Ethereum ecosystem.

Cronos also supports the Cosmos Network's inter-blockchain communication (IBC) protocol, which enables cross-chain communication and interoperability between different blockchain networks. This allows Cronos to support a wider range of use cases and applications, making it a more versatile and flexible platform for developers and users.

Cronos has already attracted significant interest from the blockchain and cryptocurrency community, with a growing ecosystem of developers, projects, and applications being built on the platform. With its focus on scalability, interoperability, and compatibility with the Ethereum ecosystem, Cronos has the potential to become a major player in the decentralized application space in the years to come.

Overall, Cronos is a promising layer 2 solution for Ethereum that offers fast, scalable, and cost-effective infrastructure for decentralized applications and other use cases. With its support for the Ethereum Virtual Machine, the Cosmos Network's IBC protocol, and its growing ecosystem of developers and projects, Cronos has the potential to become a key player in the blockchain and cryptocurrency industry.

Chapter 35

Lido DAO (LDO)

Lido DAO (LDO) is a decentralized autonomous organization that operates a stakepool for Ethereum 2.0. Launched in 2020, Lido aims to make staking on Ethereum 2.0 more accessible and secure for users by allowing them to stake their ETH without having to run their own validator node.

Lido operates by pooling ETH from users and then staking it on the Ethereum 2.0 network through a network of validators. Lido's validators are distributed across multiple geographies and are designed to provide a high degree of security and reliability. Users who stake their ETH with Lido receive stETH tokens in return, which represent their share of the total pool of staked ETH.

One of the key benefits of staking with Lido is that users can stake any amount of ETH, regardless of whether it meets the minimum threshold required to run a validator node. This makes staking on Ethereum 2.0 more accessible for smaller holders, who may not have the technical expertise or resources to run their own validator node.

Lido also offers a range of additional benefits for stakers, including the ability to earn rewards in the form of additional stETH tokens and the ability to participate in Lido's governance process. Lido DAO is governed by a decentralized community of stakeholders who can propose and vote on changes to the protocol. This ensures that Lido is operated in a transparent and decentralized manner, with the interests of the community at the forefront.

Lido has become one of the most popular options for staking on Ethereum 2.0, with over $8 billion worth of ETH currently staked through the Lido protocol. Lido's success is a testament to the growing demand for decentralized stakepools and the importance of accessibility and security in the DeFi space.

Overall, Lido DAO is a promising project that has the potential to play a key role in the growth and adoption of Ethereum 2.0. By providing an accessible and secure way for users to stake their ETH, Lido is helping to make Ethereum 2.0 more decentralized and accessible for all.

Chapter 36

Arbitrum (ARB)

Arbitrum (ARB) is a layer 2 scaling solution for Ethereum that aims to address the scalability issues of the Ethereum network. Launched in 2021, Arbitrum uses an innovative approach to achieve high scalability and low transaction fees, making it an attractive option for developers and users alike.

Arbitrum operates as a sidechain to the Ethereum network, which means that it runs in parallel to the main Ethereum chain. However, unlike other sidechains, Arbitrum is designed to be fully compatible with the Ethereum Virtual Machine (EVM), which is the underlying technology that powers the Ethereum network. This means that developers can easily port their Ethereum-based applications to Arbitrum without having to make any significant changes to their code.

Arbitrum uses a technique called optimistic rollups to achieve high scalability and low transaction fees. In simple terms, optimistic rollups allow users to conduct transactions off-chain, with the results of those transactions only being posted to the Ethereum network when necessary. This reduces the burden on the Ethereum network and allows for faster and cheaper transactions.

One of the key benefits of Arbitrum is that it offers a high degree of security and decentralization. Unlike other layer 2 scaling solutions, Arbitrum uses a decentralized network of validators to process transactions, which helps to ensure that the network remains secure and resistant to attacks.

Arbitrum has already gained significant traction in the Ethereum community, with a number of high-profile projects, such as Uniswap and SushiSwap, already deploying their applications on the Arbitrum network. This is a testament to the scalability and usability of the platform, as well as its potential to drive the growth and adoption of decentralized finance (DeFi) applications.

In addition to its scalability benefits, Arbitrum also offers a number of other advantages for developers and users, including lower gas fees, faster transaction times, and improved user experience. These benefits make Arbitrum an attractive option for anyone looking to build or use decentralized applications on the Ethereum network.

Overall, Arbitrum is a promising project that has the potential to play a significant role in the growth and adoption of decentralized applications on the Ethereum network. By offering a scalable, secure, and user-friendly platform for developers and users, Arbitrum is helping to drive the evolution of decentralized finance and the wider blockchain ecosystem.

Chapter 37

Near Protocol (NEAR)

Near Protocol (NEAR) is a decentralized blockchain platform that aims to provide a scalable and developer-friendly infrastructure for building decentralized applications (dApps). Launched in 2018, NEAR is designed to address the scalability and usability issues faced by existing blockchain platforms, such as Ethereum.

NEAR uses a unique consensus mechanism called Nightshade, which combines the benefits of sharding and proof-of-stake (PoS) to achieve high scalability and throughput while maintaining a high degree of security and decentralization. The Nightshade consensus mechanism divides the network into smaller groups of nodes, or shards, each of which processes a subset of transactions. This allows NEAR to process a large number of transactions in parallel, significantly increasing the network's throughput.

NEAR also offers a number of features that make it an attractive option for developers. These include:

- NEAR SDK: A software development kit (SDK) that allows developers to build and deploy dApps on the NEAR network using familiar programming languages, such as Rust and AssemblyScript.

- NEAR Wallet: A non-custodial wallet that allows users to store and manage their NEAR tokens and interact with dApps on the NEAR network.

- NEAR Explorer: A blockchain explorer that allows users to view and track transactions on the NEAR network in real-time.

In addition to these features, NEAR also has a strong focus on user experience (UX) and usability. This includes features such as easy onboarding for new users, a user-friendly developer environment, and seamless integration with existing web2.0 technologies.

NEAR has already gained significant traction in the blockchain community, with a number of high-profile projects, such as Paraswap and Mintbase, already deploying their dApps on the NEAR network. This is a testament to the scalability and usability of the platform, as well as its potential to drive the growth and adoption of decentralized applications.

NEAR has also received significant investment from top-tier venture capital firms, such as Andreessen Horowitz, which has led several funding rounds for the project.

In conclusion, NEAR is a promising blockchain platform that offers a scalable and developer-friendly infrastructure for building decentralized applications. With its unique consensus mechanism, focus on user experience, and strong support from the blockchain community, NEAR has the potential to drive the evolution of decentralized finance (DeFi) and other blockchain-based applications.

Chapter 38

V

VeChain (VET)

VeChain (VET) is a decentralized blockchain platform that specializes in supply chain management and business solutions. Launched in 2015, VeChain aims to improve supply chain transparency, reduce costs, and enhance efficiency by providing a tamper-proof and traceable ledger for tracking goods and services.

VeChain uses a unique two-token system, which includes VeChain Token (VET) and VeChainThor Energy (VTHO). VET is used for staking, transactions, and smart contract execution, while VTHO is used as a gas fee to power transactions and smart contracts.

One of the key features of VeChain is its focus on enterprise solutions. VeChain provides a range of services and tools for businesses, including:

- VeChain ToolChain: A comprehensive platform for businesses to digitize and manage their supply chain processes, including product lifecycle management, data management, and business intelligence.

- VeChain Sync: A mobile app that allows businesses to easily access and manage their supply chain data on the go.

- VeChain Authority Masternodes: A network of nodes that provide governance and consensus services to the VeChain network, ensuring its security and decentralization.

VeChain also has partnerships with a number of high-profile companies, including PwC, Walmart China, BMW, and LVMH, among others. These partnerships demonstrate the potential of VeChain's technology to transform supply chain management and business operations across a range of industries.

VeChain has also gained significant traction in the blockchain community, with a market capitalization of over $12 billion at the time of writing. This is a testament to the value and potential of VeChain's technology, as well as its ability to address real-world problems.

In addition to its focus on enterprise solutions, VeChain also has a strong commitment to sustainability and environmental responsibility. VeChain has partnered with organizations such as DNV GL and the World Wildlife Fund (WWF) to develop blockchain solutions for tracking and verifying sustainable practices in supply chains.

In conclusion, VeChain is a promising blockchain platform that specializes in supply chain management and business solutions. With its unique two-token system, focus on enterprise solutions, and commitment to sustainability, VeChain has the potential to transform supply chains and business operations across a range of industries. As

Chapter 39

ApeCoin (APE)

ApeCoin (APE) is a community-driven cryptocurrency that was launched in April 2021 as a meme coin. ApeCoin is a decentralized finance (DeFi) token built on the Binance Smart Chain (BSC) and aims to provide a fun and engaging experience for its community members while also creating opportunities for investors to earn rewards through staking and yield farming.

One of the unique features of ApeCoin is its focus on community involvement and engagement. The ApeCoin community is active and passionate, with members coming together to create memes, artwork, and other content to promote the project. ApeCoin also has a strong social media presence, with active communities on Twitter, Reddit, and Discord.

In addition to its community-driven approach, ApeCoin also offers a range of staking and yield farming opportunities for investors. ApeCoin holders can stake their tokens to earn rewards in the form of more APE tokens. There are also opportunities for yield farming, which involves providing liquidity to ApeSwap, the decentralized exchange (DEX) built on the Binance Smart Chain that ApeCoin is associated with.

ApeCoin has also been making strides in developing its ecosystem and partnerships. In May 2021, ApeCoin announced a partnership with ChainGuardian, a blockchain-based gaming platform, to integrate APE tokens into ChainGuardian's games. This partnership is expected to expand the use cases and adoption of APE tokens beyond just the DeFi space.

While ApeCoin is still a relatively new and experimental project, it has gained a significant following and has a market capitalization of over $100 million at the time of writing. This demonstrates the potential of meme coins to attract communities and investors and to create innovative and engaging experiences.

In conclusion, ApeCoin is a community-driven meme coin that offers a unique and engaging experience for its members. With its focus on community involvement and participation, as well as its range of staking and yield farming opportunities, ApeCoin has the potential to grow and develop into a successful project. As ApeCoin continues to evolve and expand its ecosystem and partnerships, it will be interesting to see how it contributes to the broader DeFi and blockchain landscape.

Chapter 40

Quant (QNT)

Quant (QNT) is a blockchain project that aims to connect various blockchain networks and businesses. The goal of the project is to create a unified platform that allows businesses to operate on different blockchain networks seamlessly. Quant is built on the Overledger technology, which is a blockchain operating system that connects different blockchains.

Quant's main focus is on creating an ecosystem that enables cross-chain communication, interoperability, and collaboration among various blockchain networks. The project's ultimate goal is to build a global blockchain operating system that connects all networks and devices.

One of the key features of Quant is its multi-chain architecture, which allows the project to support different blockchain networks. This architecture allows businesses to access and use different blockchain networks without having to worry about interoperability issues. By leveraging the Overledger technology, Quant can create a seamless and secure bridge between different blockchain networks.

Quant's ecosystem includes various products and services, including the Overledger Network, which is a decentralized network that connects different blockchain networks. The network enables interoperability between different blockchains and allows developers to create decentralized applications (dApps) that operate across different networks.

Another product offered by Quant is the Quant Developer Portal, which provides developers with tools and resources to build decentralized applications that can interact with various blockchain networks. The portal provides access to APIs, SDKs, and other tools that make it easier to create dApps that can operate on multiple networks.

Quant also has its native cryptocurrency, QNT, which is used as a utility token within the ecosystem. QNT can be used to pay for transaction fees, access various services and products, and participate in the governance of the network.

At the time of writing, Quant has a market capitalization of over $1 billion and is listed on several major cryptocurrency exchanges. The project has also attracted partnerships with various businesses and organizations, including SIA, the leading European payment infrastructure and technology company, and the United Nations.

In conclusion, Quant is a blockchain project that aims to connect different blockchain networks and businesses through its multi-chain architecture and Overledger technology. With its focus on interoperability and collaboration, Quant has the potential to create a global blockchain operating system that connects all networks and devices. As Quant continues to develop and expand its ecosystem, it will be interesting to see how it contributes to the broader blockchain and business landscape.

Chapter 41

Algorand (ALGO)

Algorand (ALGO) is a blockchain platform that was created with the goal of providing a secure, scalable, and decentralized infrastructure for building decentralized applications (dApps) and issuing digital assets. It was founded by Silvio Micali, a computer science professor at MIT and recipient of the Turing Award, in 2017.

Algorand's main focus is on achieving high transaction throughput, with a capacity of up to 1,000 transactions per second (TPS) on the mainnet. This is made possible through the use of a pure proof-of-stake (PPoS) consensus algorithm that allows for fast confirmation times and low transaction fees.

PPoS is a variation of the proof-of-stake (PoS) consensus algorithm, in which block validators are chosen randomly and in a way that is proportional to the amount of ALGO they hold. This means that the more ALGO a validator holds, the more likely they are to be chosen to validate the next block. Validators are incentivized to act honestly by receiving a portion of the transaction fees as well as newly minted ALGO as rewards.

Algorand also offers several features that make it an attractive platform for developers. It has a smart contract language called TEAL (Transaction Execution Approval Language) that is designed to be easy to learn and use, and can be used to create complex smart contracts that can execute in milliseconds. Additionally, Algorand supports the creation of fungible and non-fungible tokens (NFTs) on its platform, which can be used for a wide range of applications such as loyalty programs, gaming assets, and art.

One of the unique features of Algorand is its commitment to decentralization. Unlike many other blockchain platforms that have a central governing body or foundation, Algorand has a fully decentralized governance model. This means that all ALGO holders can participate in decision-making processes, such as protocol upgrades and changes to the platform's governance structure, by submitting and voting on proposals.

In terms of adoption, Algorand has seen significant growth in recent years. It has partnerships with a number of companies, including Circle, USDC, and Tether, which have all launched stablecoins on the Algorand blockchain. Additionally, the government of El Salvador has announced that it will be using the Algorand blockchain to build its national digital currency, the Chivo wallet.

In conclusion, Algorand is a promising blockchain platform that offers high transaction throughput, low fees, and easy-to-use smart contracts. Its commitment to decentralization and partnerships with leading companies in the blockchain industry make it an attractive option for developers and investors alike.

Chapter 42

Fantom (FTM)

Fantom (FTM) is a fast and scalable blockchain platform that aims to provide high-speed, low-cost transactions and smart contract functionality. The platform was launched in 2018 and has gained significant attention in the blockchain community for its innovative approach to solving some of the key issues that have hampered the adoption of blockchain technology.

Fantom uses a Directed Acyclic Graph (DAG) consensus algorithm, which is designed to achieve high transaction speeds and scalability. In a DAG-based system, transactions are not grouped into blocks, but instead are confirmed individually by the network. This allows for faster transaction confirmation times and a higher throughput compared to traditional blockchain systems.

One of the key features of Fantom is its smart contract platform, which is built using the Ethereum Virtual Machine (EVM) and is fully compatible with Ethereum smart contracts. This allows developers to easily migrate their existing smart contracts to the Fantom platform, making it easier to build decentralized applications (dApps) that are compatible with both Ethereum and Fantom.

Another important feature of Fantom is its support for multiple consensus algorithms. In addition to the DAG consensus algorithm, the platform also supports a variant of the Practical Byzantine Fault Tolerance (PBFT) consensus algorithm, which is used in traditional blockchains like Ethereum. This allows Fantom to offer a flexible and customizable consensus model that can adapt to different use cases and transaction volumes.

In terms of adoption, Fantom has seen significant growth in recent years. The platform has partnered with a number of companies, including Binance and Chainlink, to expand its reach and offer additional services to users. Additionally, the Fantom Foundation has launched several initiatives to support the development of the Fantom ecosystem, including a developer grant program and a liquidity mining program to incentivize users to participate in the network.

Fantom has also gained attention for its work in the DeFi (decentralized finance) space. The platform offers a range of DeFi applications, including a decentralized exchange (DEX) and a yield farming platform, which allows users to earn rewards for providing liquidity to the network.

In conclusion, Fantom is a fast and scalable blockchain platform that offers a flexible and customizable consensus model and is fully compatible with Ethereum smart contracts. Its growing ecosystem and partnerships with leading companies in the blockchain industry make it an attractive option for developers and investors looking to build decentralized applications and participate in the DeFi space.

Chapter 43

The Graph (GRT)

The Graph (GRT) is a decentralized protocol that enables developers to easily query and index data from blockchain networks. The protocol was launched in 2018 and has gained significant attention in the blockchain community for its innovative approach to indexing and querying blockchain data.

The Graph uses a decentralized network of nodes, called Indexers, to index data from blockchain networks. Indexers are incentivized to provide accurate and timely data by receiving fees from developers who query their data. Developers, in turn, are able to easily access and query blockchain data using a simple API interface.

One of the key features of The Graph is its subgraph technology, which allows developers to define custom data models and query them using GraphQL, a query language for APIs. Subgraphs can be created for any type of data on a blockchain, including transactions, events, and token balances. This allows developers to easily access and analyze blockchain data in a way that is more intuitive and efficient than traditional methods.

Another important feature of The Graph is its support for multiple blockchain networks, including Ethereum, IPFS, and Avalanche. This allows developers to easily index and query data from multiple blockchain networks using a single API interface.

In terms of adoption, The Graph has seen significant growth in recent years. The protocol has partnerships with a number of leading blockchain projects, including Uniswap, Aave, and Chainlink, which have all integrated with The Graph to improve their data indexing and querying capabilities. Additionally, the protocol has launched several initiatives to support the development of the ecosystem, including a grant program and a data challenge program to incentivize developers to create subgraphs for new blockchain networks and data types.

The Graph has also gained attention for its work in the DeFi (decentralized finance) space. The protocol offers a range of DeFi applications, including a decentralized exchange (DEX) and a yield farming platform, which allows users to earn rewards for providing liquidity to the network.

In conclusion, The Graph is a decentralized protocol that enables developers to easily index and query data from blockchain networks using a simple API interface. Its subgraph technology and support for multiple blockchain networks make it an attractive option for developers looking to access and analyze blockchain data in a more efficient and intuitive way. With a growing ecosystem and partnerships with leading blockchain projects, The Graph is well-positioned to play an important role in the future of blockchain data indexing and querying.

Chapter 44

Chiliz (CHZ)

Chiliz is a blockchain-based platform that allows sports and entertainment organizations to create fan engagement and monetization opportunities through the use of non-fungible tokens (NFTs) and fan tokens. The platform is built on the Ethereum blockchain and uses smart contracts to enable secure and transparent transactions.

One of the key features of Chiliz is its focus on fan engagement and monetization. The platform allows sports and entertainment organizations to create fan tokens, which are unique NFTs that represent a specific fan's ownership and participation in the organization. Fan tokens can be used for a variety of purposes, including access to exclusive content, merchandise discounts, and voting rights on team decisions.

Another important feature of Chiliz is its focus on user experience. The platform provides a range of tools and resources for organizations to create engaging fan experiences and drive fan participation. This includes a mobile app called Socios.com, which allows fans to buy, sell, and trade fan tokens, as well as participate in team decisions through a voting system.

Chiliz has also gained attention for its partnerships with leading sports and entertainment organizations. The platform has formed partnerships with a range of global sports teams and leagues, including FC Barcelona, Paris Saint-Germain, and the UFC. These partnerships have helped to drive adoption of Chiliz and fan tokens, as well as increase engagement and monetization opportunities for these organizations.

In terms of adoption, Chiliz has seen significant growth since its launch in 2018. The platform has a growing ecosystem of sports and entertainment organizations, as well as a large and active community of fans and users. Chiliz has also received support from a number of leading blockchain investors and organizations, including Binance and Hashed.

In conclusion, Chiliz is a blockchain-based platform that allows sports and entertainment organizations to create fan engagement and monetization opportunities through the use of NFTs and fan tokens. Its focus on fan engagement, user experience, and partnerships with leading sports and entertainment organizations make it an attractive option for fans and organizations looking to participate in the blockchain ecosystem. As the use of blockchain in the sports and entertainment industry continues to evolve, Chiliz is well-positioned to play an important role in shaping the future of fan engagement and monetization.

Chapter 45

EOS (EOS)

EOS is a blockchain platform designed to provide a high-performance infrastructure for decentralized applications (dApps) and smart contracts. The platform was launched in 2018 by Block.one, a blockchain technology company based in the Cayman Islands.

One of the key features of EOS is its delegated proof-of-stake (DPoS) consensus algorithm. In a DPoS system, block producers are elected by token holders to validate transactions and create new blocks. This allows for faster transaction speeds and higher throughput compared to traditional proof-of-work (PoW) systems like Bitcoin.

EOS also offers a unique governance model, which allows token holders to vote on changes to the network and the allocation of resources. This provides a more democratic and decentralized approach to network governance, as opposed to a centralized decision-making process.

Another important feature of EOS is its smart contract platform, which is built using the Web Assembly (WASM) standard. This allows for more efficient and secure smart contract execution, as well as compatibility with multiple programming languages. EOS smart contracts can also be upgraded without requiring a hard fork, which can improve the efficiency of the network.

In terms of adoption, EOS has seen significant growth in recent years. The platform has attracted a number of notable dApps, including decentralized exchanges (DEXs), social networks, and gaming platforms. Additionally, the EOS ecosystem has a strong developer community and a range of developer tools, including a software development kit (SDK) and a web-based integrated development environment (IDE).

EOS has also gained attention for its work in the DeFi (decentralized finance) space. The platform offers a range of DeFi applications, including stablecoins, lending platforms, and liquidity pools, which allow users to earn rewards for providing liquidity to the network.

In conclusion, EOS is a high-performance blockchain platform that offers a unique governance model and a scalable and secure smart contract platform. Its growing ecosystem and partnerships with leading blockchain projects make it an attractive option for developers and investors looking to build decentralized applications and participate in the DeFi space. While the platform has faced some criticism over its governance and centralization, it remains one of the most popular blockchain platforms in the industry.

Chapter 46

The Sandbox (SAND)

The Sandbox (SAND) is a decentralized gaming platform built on the Ethereum blockchain. The platform allows users to create, share, and monetize their own gaming experiences using non-fungible tokens (NFTs) and a proprietary game development platform.

One of the key features of The Sandbox is its virtual world, which allows users to create and interact with 3D gaming environments. The virtual world is divided into LAND parcels, which can be purchased and owned by users. These LAND parcels can then be used to create and publish games and other interactive experiences.

The Sandbox also offers a game development platform, which allows users to easily create and publish their own games using a drag-and-drop interface. This makes game development accessible to a wider audience, including those without coding experience.

Another important feature of The Sandbox is its integration with NFTs.

Each LAND parcel and game asset is represented as an NFT, which allows for unique ownership and transferability. This also enables creators to monetize their games and assets by selling them on various marketplaces.

In terms of adoption, The Sandbox has seen significant growth in recent years. The platform has partnerships with a number of leading blockchain projects, including Binance, Animoca Brands, and Atari, which have all integrated with The Sandbox to improve their gaming experiences and NFT offerings. Additionally, The Sandbox has launched several initiatives to support the development of the ecosystem, including a grant program and a creator fund to incentivize developers to create and publish games on the platform.

The Sandbox has also gained attention for its work in the NFT space. The platform offers a range of NFTs, including LAND parcels, game assets, and virtual wearables, which have become popular among collectors and gamers alike. The Sandbox has also launched several high-profile partnerships with brands and celebrities, including Care Bears and Deadmau5, to create unique NFT collections and experiences.

In conclusion, The Sandbox is a decentralized gaming platform that allows users to create, share, and monetize their own gaming experiences using NFTs and a proprietary game development platform. Its virtual world and easy-to-use game development tools make it an attractive option for creators and gamers looking to participate in the blockchain gaming space. With a growing ecosystem and partnerships with leading blockchain projects, The Sandbox is well-positioned to play an important role in the future of blockchain gaming and NFTs.

Chapter 47

BitDAO (BIT)

BitDAO is a decentralized autonomous organization (DAO) that aims to accelerate the adoption of decentralized finance (DeFi) and blockchain technology. The platform is built on the Ethereum blockchain and uses smart contracts to enable transparent and decentralized decision-making among its members.

One of the key features of BitDAO is its focus on community governance. The platform allows anyone to become a member by holding its native cryptocurrency, BIT. Members have the ability to propose and vote on decisions related to the direction and operation of the organization, including the allocation of funds for research and development, partnerships, and investments.

Another important feature of BitDAO is its focus on supporting and investing in promising blockchain projects. The platform has a dedicated investment arm, called BitDAO Ventures, which provides funding and support for early-stage blockchain startups. BitDAO also partners with leading blockchain investors and organizations to identify and support promising projects in the industry.

In terms of technology, BitDAO has developed a range of tools and resources to support its mission. This includes a decentralized exchange (DEX) called BitSwap, which allows for trustless and secure trading of cryptocurrencies and other digital assets. BitDAO is also exploring the development of new DeFi products and services, such as decentralized insurance and lending platforms.

BitDAO has gained attention for its large and active community, as well as its partnerships with leading blockchain investors and organizations. The platform has received support from some of the most well-known names in the industry, including Peter Thiel, Founders Fund, and Pantera Capital. This support has helped to drive adoption of BitDAO and its mission to accelerate the adoption of blockchain technology.

In terms of adoption, BitDAO is still in its early stages, but the platform has already demonstrated significant potential. The platform has a growing community of members and supporters, as well as a range of partnerships and investments in promising blockchain projects. BitDAO is well-positioned to play an important role in shaping the future of DeFi and blockchain technology.

In conclusion, BitDAO is a decentralized autonomous organization that aims to accelerate the adoption of DeFi and blockchain technology. Its focus on community governance, investment in promising blockchain projects, and development of new DeFi products and services make it an attractive option for anyone looking to participate in the blockchain ecosystem. As the adoption of blockchain technology continues to accelerate, BitDAO is well-positioned to play an important role in shaping the future of DeFi and decentralized organizations.

Chapter 48

Aave (AAVE)

Aave is a decentralized finance (DeFi) platform built on the Ethereum blockchain. The platform allows users to borrow and lend cryptocurrencies without the need for a traditional intermediary such as a bank. Aave is one of the leading DeFi protocols in the industry and has gained significant adoption since its launch in 2020.

One of the key features of Aave is its use of a liquidity pool model for lending and borrowing. In this model, users can deposit cryptocurrencies into a pool, which is then used to fund loans for other users. Users who deposit their assets into the pool are then rewarded with interest on their deposits, while borrowers pay interest on the loans they receive. Aave also offers a range of features, including flash loans, which allow users to borrow assets for a short period of time without collateral, and credit delegation, which allows users to delegate their credit lines to other users.

Another important feature of Aave is its focus on user control and governance. The platform is governed by Aave token holders, who can vote on changes to the protocol, including fee changes and new features. This provides a more decentralized and community-driven approach to governance, as opposed to a centralized decision-making process.

Aave has also gained attention for its work in the DeFi space. The platform offers a range of DeFi applications, including stablecoins, collateralized loans, and flash loans, which allow users to earn rewards and access liquidity without the need for traditional financial intermediaries. Additionally, Aave has partnerships with a number of leading blockchain projects, including Polygon and Chainlink, which have all integrated with Aave to improve their DeFi offerings.

In terms of adoption, Aave has seen significant growth in recent years. The platform has over $10 billion in total value locked (TVL) and has become one of the largest and most popular DeFi protocols in the industry. Aave also has a growing ecosystem and developer community, with a range of tools and resources available to developers looking to build on the platform.

In conclusion, Aave is a decentralized finance platform that allows users to borrow and lend cryptocurrencies without the need for a traditional intermediary. Its focus on user control and governance, as well as its range of DeFi applications and partnerships, make it an attractive option for investors and users looking to participate in the DeFi space. As the DeFi industry continues to grow, Aave is well-positioned to play an important role in shaping the future of decentralized finance.

Chapter 49

Stacks (STX)

Stacks is a blockchain platform that allows developers to build decentralized applications (dApps) on top of the Bitcoin blockchain. Unlike other blockchain platforms, Stacks is designed to be compatible with Bitcoin, which is the world's most widely used and recognized cryptocurrency. This makes it easier for developers to build dApps that can leverage the security and stability of the Bitcoin network.

One of the key features of Stacks is its ability to allow developers to build smart contracts on top of the Bitcoin blockchain. This allows for the creation of decentralized applications that are more secure and transparent than traditional web applications. Stacks also provides a range of tools and resources for developers, including an open-source development kit (SDK), which includes a smart contract language called Clarity.

Another important feature of Stacks is its focus on user-owned data and identity. The platform allows users to own and control their data, which can be used to authenticate their identity across different dApps. This provides a more secure and private approach to identity verification, as opposed to traditional methods that rely on centralized providers.

Stacks has also gained attention for its innovative approach to blockchain governance. The platform uses a unique consensus mechanism called Proof-of-Transfer (PoX), which allows Stacks token holders to vote on changes to the network. PoX also allows Bitcoin miners to earn Stacks tokens by locking up Bitcoin in the Stacks network. This creates a symbiotic relationship between the Stacks and Bitcoin networks, which helps to increase the security and stability of both platforms.

In terms of adoption, Stacks has seen steady growth since its launch in 2018. The platform has a growing ecosystem of dApps and developers, with a range of applications already built on top of the Stacks blockchain. Stacks has also received support from a number of leading blockchain investors and organizations, including Winklevoss Capital and Blockchain.com.

In conclusion, Stacks is a blockchain platform that allows developers to build decentralized applications on top of the Bitcoin blockchain. Its focus on smart contracts, user-owned data and identity, and innovative blockchain governance make it an attractive option for developers and users looking to participate in the blockchain ecosystem. As the blockchain industry continues to evolve, Stacks is well-positioned to play an important role in shaping the future of decentralized applications and blockchain technology.

Chapter 50

Decentraland (MANA)

Decentraland is a virtual world built on the Ethereum blockchain that allows users to create, experience, and monetize content and applications in a decentralized manner. The platform uses blockchain technology to enable true ownership of virtual land, giving users the ability to create and monetize unique experiences and applications within the virtual world.

One of the key features of Decentraland is its use of non-fungible tokens (NFTs) to represent virtual land ownership. Users can purchase virtual land using the platform's native cryptocurrency, MANA, and can then build and create whatever they can imagine within their virtual property. This creates a unique and diverse virtual world, where users can explore different environments and experiences created by other users.

Another important feature of Decentraland is its focus on user-generated content and experiences. The platform provides a range of tools and resources for developers and content creators to build and monetize their creations within the virtual world. This includes a decentralized marketplace where users can buy and sell virtual assets, as well as a scripting language called Solidity, which allows developers to build interactive experiences and applications.

Decentraland has also gained attention for its use of decentralized governance. The platform is governed by a decentralized autonomous organization (DAO), which allows MANA holders to vote on changes to the platform, including development proposals and policy changes. This provides a more democratic and community-driven approach to governance, as opposed to a centralized decision-making process.

In terms of adoption, Decentraland has seen significant growth since its launch in 2017. The platform has a growing ecosystem of developers and content creators, with a range of applications and experiences already built within the virtual world. Decentraland has also received support from a number of leading blockchain investors and organizations, including Andreessen Horowitz and Coinbase Ventures.

In conclusion, Decentraland is a virtual world built on the Ethereum blockchain that allows users to create, experience, and monetize content and applications in a decentralized manner. Its focus on virtual land ownership, user-generated content, and decentralized governance make it an attractive option for users looking to participate in the blockchain ecosystem. As the virtual world industry continues to evolve, Decentraland is well-positioned to play an important role in shaping the future of virtual experiences and decentralized applications.

Chapter 51

Tips to Keep In Mind

Building wealth in cryptocurrency can be a risky endeavor, but if done correctly, it can also be very rewarding. Here are some tips to keep in mind:

1. Do your own research: Before investing in any cryptocurrency, it's important to do your due diligence and research the project thoroughly. Look into the team behind the project, the technology, and the potential use cases. This will help you make informed investment decisions.

2. Diversify your portfolio: Just like with traditional investments, it's important to diversify your cryptocurrency portfolio. Don't put all your eggs in one basket instead, consider investing in a variety of projects to spread out your risk.

3. Take a long-term approach: Cryptocurrencies can be volatile in the short term, but over the long term, they have shown impressive returns. If you're looking to build wealth in cryptocurrency, consider taking a long-term approach and holding onto your investments for several years.

4. Use dollar-cost averaging: Instead of investing a lump sum all at

once, consider using dollar-cost averaging. This involves investing a fixed amount of money at regular intervals, which can help smooth out the impact of market volatility.

5. Stay informed: The cryptocurrency market is constantly changing, so it's important to stay informed about the latest developments. Follow news outlets, social media, and industry experts to stay up-to-date on the latest trends and developments in the crypto world.

Remember, building wealth in cryptocurrency is not a guaranteed endeavor, and it's important to invest only what you can afford to lose. Always exercise caution and make informed investment decisions. I hope you did learn a thing or two from reading this book.

Best of luck on your crypto journey!